GW00778535

the
Spirit
of
Beauty

the Spirit of Beauty

Van Cleef & Arpels

ÉDITIONS
XAVIER
BARRAL

BEAUTY IS LIFE. And life is time passing by, with its springtimes and winters, joys and solitudes, sorrows and celebrations... Beauty is composed of all these moments, it is alive, pulsating, above all not stationary, frozen in a position or restricted to aesthetic values which each era loves to reinvent anyway. Beauty is like a flower. In order to blossom, it can count on staunch allies: love, of course, but also intelligence, curiosity, talent, and imagination. Of course, beauty loves to take the limelight, the cinema seems to have been created in its honour. In the eye of the lens, it can be moving, solemn, insolent; sometimes it is even brave enough to risk offending. Directors know it well. They know that it is not unswervingly connected to youth, but to elegance, grace... some would say nobility of the heart. We actresses prefer to leave it unnamed, believing that it is a daily gift and that if time takes it away from us, it gives us in exchange the freedom to look it in the eye and say, "I look good today, don't you think?"

Beauty loves to be light-hearted, to pick a rose or an iris, softly sing a song, choose a piece of jewellery. It is on that note that Beauty is invited to Van Cleef & Arpels: to act as muse and oversee the appearance of a multitude of jewellery creations. The jeweller has always welcomed it with discretion and talent, with that inimitable style that has made it famous, and won over so many women (and their sweethearts) throughout the world. This exhibition testifies to this. In amazing creations of gold and precious stones, beauty is transformed into a gift. Into a tribute... to beauty!

Catherine DENEUVE

Spirit of Nature

FROM ANCIENT times to today, nature has provided the most fertile source for jewelry designers. Whether portrayed stylistically or naturalistically, plants and animals have been depicted in various degrees of artfulness but it was in the twentieth century that Van Cleef & Arpels took the imagery to new heights, creating flora and fauna that have become icons of their time.

Relatively soon after their founding in 1906, they created a lifelike grape bunch with diamond-set leaves and natural pearl grapes in different color gradations to differentiate each individual fruit; a subtle detail but one that only a discerning designer would conceive. The grapes are so realistically rendered they appear as if they could be picked from the bunch.

The Art Deco period of the 1920s was characterized by geometric configurations. Van Cleef & Arpels interpreted this style by abstracting floral motifs to give the impression of a flower such as the blossoms on a vanity case that are reinterpretations of forget-me-nots, a familiar flower in jewelry design from the late nineteenth century.

By the 1930s, flowers were created as if freshly picked from the garden as epitomized in a bouquet of violets with each blossom carved from an amethyst with the gold stems held together by a gold ribbon. Perhaps the most inventive and most magnificent of Van Cleef & Arpels' floral jewelry is the peony clip brooch; the flower based on the Japanese version of the bloom. The flower was so highly regarded in Japan it was called, "The King of Flowers." The clip brooch is created in the Mystery Set technique, a painstaking procedure in which 700 square-cut rubies are mounted into a three-dimensional grid, with the resulting effect simulating the actual flower. Each ruby is perfectly matched and individually cut so that, when mounted, replicate both the color and curvature of the petals. Attention to detail is also evident on the diamond-set leaves where the veins are cut out of the metal leaving open spaces and providing a counterbalance to the compactness of the design. This brooch is a *tour-de-force* of design and workmanship and ranks among the foremost jewels of the last century. It was originally part of a double clip brooch, ordered by a royal family.

Van Cleef & Arpels created not only important jewels but also ones that were fun, fun to look at and fun to wear. Not many jewelry maisons would turn to the mushroom for inspiration but, in 1968, Van Cleef & Arpels created such a brooch with two caps made out of different colors of coral. Instead of portraying them in a static position with the mushrooms side by side, one stands erect while the other is canted to one side, providing movement within the design.

In the beginning of the 1940s, Louis Arpels along with designers, Maurice Duvalet and John Rubel, created a line of jewelry based on dance with ballerina brooches made up of rose-cut diamonds. The theme metamorphosed into the *libellule* fairy brooches based on the dragonfly with human features. One such brooch was made in 1944 and was part of the collection of Barbara Hutton, an important American jewelry collector. The body of the lady dragonfly is pavé-set with diamonds with rose-cut diamonds for the face, crowned with rubies. She is portrayed in the act of bestowing her magic. In her right hand, she holds a wand, made out of baguette diamonds and centered by a ruby, while rose-cut diamond and emerald wings "flutter" above her shoulders. This is a beautiful brooch but, as with all Van Cleef & Arpels' jewelry, there is something special... the rectangular diamond shapes on the wand counterbalance the round diamonds of the fairy's body, providing harmony and interest to the composition.

The avian world is captured in blissful repose in "Les Inséparables" with two love birds that almost seem to blend into one another. As with all Van Cleef & Arpels jewelry, the arrangement is cleverly conceived. The birds, perched on a branch between an assemblage of leaves on either end, look to one side with one bird glancing slightly downward, guiding the viewer's eye to the briolette diamonds hanging from the gold leaves. On another brooch, the designer has captured the essence of an alert hummingbird who twists its body while gazing in the distance, attentive to whatever is happening in its surroundings and ready to fly away if danger appears.

As the twenty-first century dawned, Van Cleef & Arpels made the commitment to continue to offer innovative jewelry to their clientele. In 2003, they introduced *The Midsummer Night's Dream High Jewelry Collection*, readapting the stories and legends of Shakespeare's play. Perhaps one of the most spectacular pieces from this collection is the *Envol* necklace, portraying the "lightness" of flight with two butterflies on opposite ends of a baguette and round diamond necklace. One is created with Mystery Set rubies with a marquise diamond for its heart and, the other, with the outline of the markings in diamonds. When worn, one butterfly lies in the hollow of the neck and the other on the neckline. It is a multi-functional jewel in which the butterflies can be detached and worn as clip brooches.

Another jewel from this collection is the *Pivoine* ring with a peony encased within tightly closed petals that, when turned, open. The ring can be worn on two fingers or, the flower head can pivot, becoming a single ring. The tradition of wearing a double band ring dates to the dynastic period in ancient Egypt and was not seen again until the turn of the twentieth century. Van Cleef & Arpels is the only jeweler today making such rings.

Throughout its history, Van Cleef & Arpels has incorporated important diamonds and gemstones into its designs. Continuing in this tradition, in 2005, they created a three-strand emerald necklace with a diamond-set floral clasp with the petals seeming to swirl around the central stone. The emeralds, formerly in the Doris Duke collection, are superb gemstones, the kind usually only seen in royal collections such as a strand from the French crown jewels in the collection of the École des Mines in Paris. To find one strand of high quality beads is rare, but to find three such strands is remarkable.

For over 100 years, Van Cleef & Arpels has created beautifully designed and impeccably made jewelry. Not satisfied on resting on their laurels, they have continued to create new and exciting jewels, not jewels of yesterday but of the twenty-first century. Its jewelry endures.

Janet ZAPATA

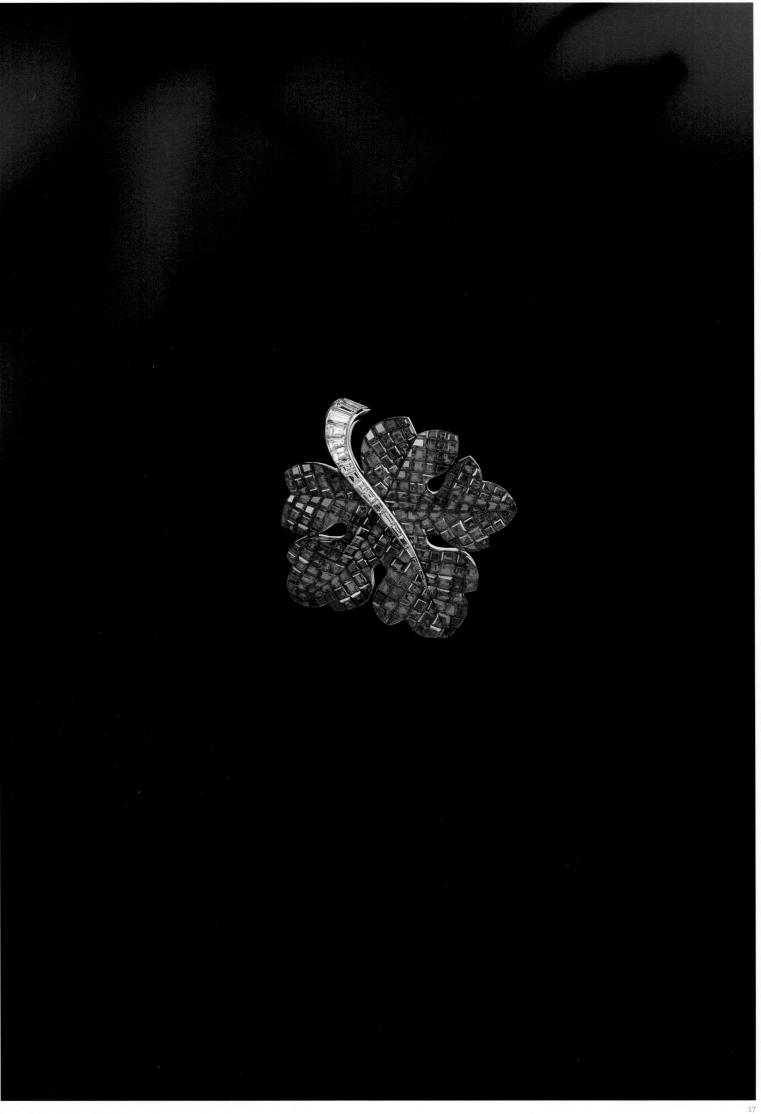

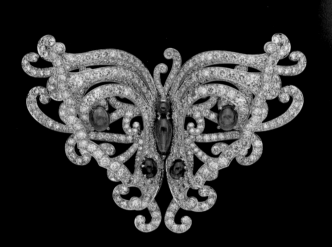

Spirit
of
Elegance

As a young jewellery specialist at Christie's, I became fascinated by the passion with which Jacques, Pierre and Claude Arpels, the owners of the House until 1999, defended the brand created by their father and uncle in 1906. An incorrect description of a Van Cleef & Arpels jewel in a Christie's catalogue ... A missing year of manufacture ... The use of the word Minaudière to describe a vanity case by another jeweller ... These inaccuracies would trigger an instant and visceral reaction, revealing a desire to preserve the ethical and historical integrity of the firm, which impressed me greatly.

But the passion behind the firm was not all. I was also intrigued by how Van Cleef & Arpels were able to influence the partnership between Haute Joaillerie and Haute Couture. Their innovative designs had taken inspiration from the technical, social and stylistic developments of the past hundred years. In turn, Van Cleef & Arpels could be credited with shaping some of these changes through their great influence on the style and fashion of the 20th century. Under the guidance of Renée Puissant, its Artistic Director between 1926 and 1942, the firm embraced every artistic and fashion trend, expressing them in jewels that were matchless in design and execution. This love affair with fashion and fabrics was continued into modern times, most notably when the firm launched its Couture Collection in 2004.

In many instances, it was the close relationships between Van Cleef & Arpels and its clients –often fashion icons in their own right– that suggested the design of new inventions. Legend has it that Charles Arpels' original idea for the Minaudière was triggered by Florence Jay Gould, the wife of American railroad magnate Frank Jay Gould. She used to carelessly fling into a Lucky Strike metal tin all the bits and pieces a society woman found indispensable. Shortly after he had observed this, Charles Arpels presented her with the first Minaudière, an unobtrusive bag which captured femininity and elegance in a practical object. It was registered as a trademark in 1933 and was the first item to feature the famous Mystery Set, which, I quickly learnt, should never be described as "Invisible setting"...

In the case of the versatile Zip necklace, it was the Duchess of Windsor who suggested in 1939 a jewel inspired by a zipper to be worn with an evening gown. Here again Van Cleef & Arpels enthusiastically captured the spirit of the time, when women were defying conventions to reach independence and freedom. As Elsa Schiaparelli appropriated the zip in the world of Haute Couture, Renée Puissant designed a piece of jewellery to celebrate this great practical invention. The first fastener could only be produced in 1950 and unsurprisingly hit the fashion world like nothing else at the time. This novel idea never lost its allure, proven again in 1988 two Zip necklaces were sold at Christie's New York for more than ten times their estimates. This probably helped encourage the firm to re-introduce it into more contemporary creations.

The inspiration behind another iconic Van Cleef & Arpels design –the Ballerina– appeared almost simultaneously, but this time in the United States. A collaboration between Maurice Duvalet, a French-born designer based in New York, Van Cleef & Arpels and John Rubel, their manufacturer, resulted in the production of these miniature gem-set figures, probably as a result of Louis Arpels' passion for the opera and ballet. This theme remained closely associated with the House and in 1967, Claude Arpels asked the Russian dancer and choreographer Balanchine to arrange a ballet called *Jewels*. The first act was an illustration of France, symbolized by emeralds; the second was about New York and the New World, represented by the vibrant red of ruby; and the last concerned Old Europe and paid homage to Imperial Russia –symbolized by the diamond!

Yet these revolutionary designs could not have been executed without great technological skills and attention to detail. These extended to the point of inventing a new alloy in 1932, when precious metals became scarce. Known as "styptor", it included a special mix of silver, aluminium, nickel and pewter, amongst others, kept as secret as the recipe for Coca Cola! Formed with the word "or" or gold and often decorated with an additional small gold element, it gave the jewelled piece an aura of chic even during years of depression and war.

Just as the relationship between Haute Couture and Haute Joaillerie is inextricably linked, so too have Christie's and Van Cleef & Arpels long shared a happy working relationship. In 2006, we were proud to collaborate with the firm on two specially curated tribute auctions organized to mark their centennial. The events were a great success with fierce bidding on all jewels, but a slight disappointment in terms of the importance of the selection offered for sale. Indeed, despite all the marketing campaigns and the efforts of our specialists to source exceptional pieces, collectors simply could not be convinced to part with their Van Cleef & Arpels jewellery. In fact, most of the responses we received were requests to bid in the auction and purchase more! This is a tribute in itself showing that even today when tastes change so fast, a Van Cleef & Arpels creation remains as daring, timeless and stylish as when it was originally created. The "Spirit of Elegance" endures forever.

François CURIEL

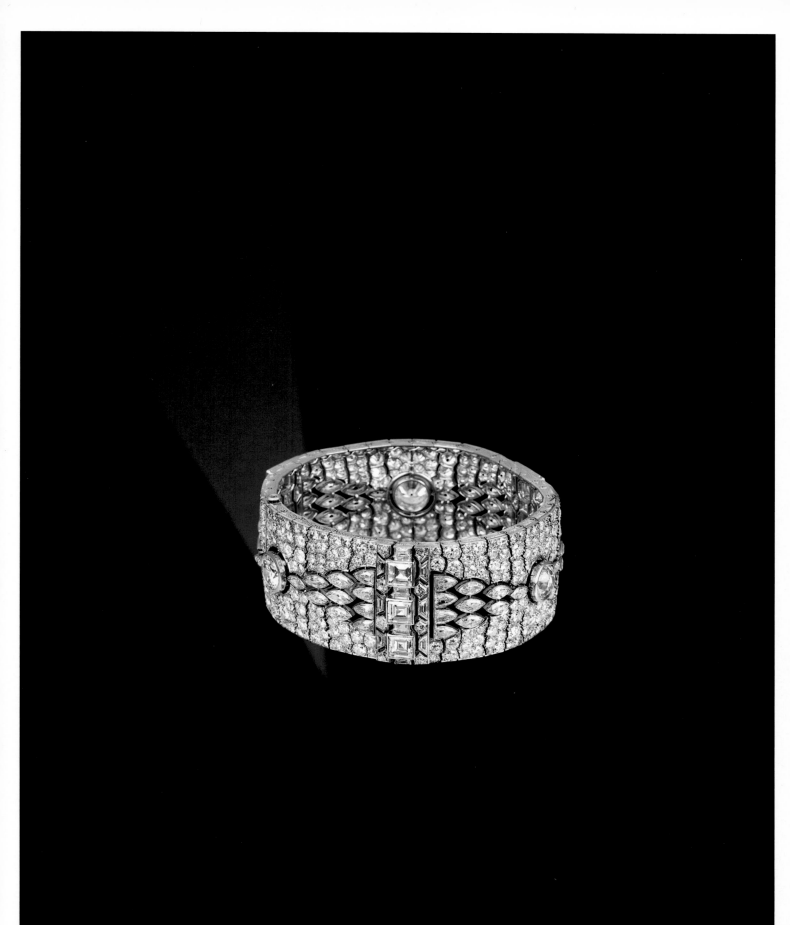

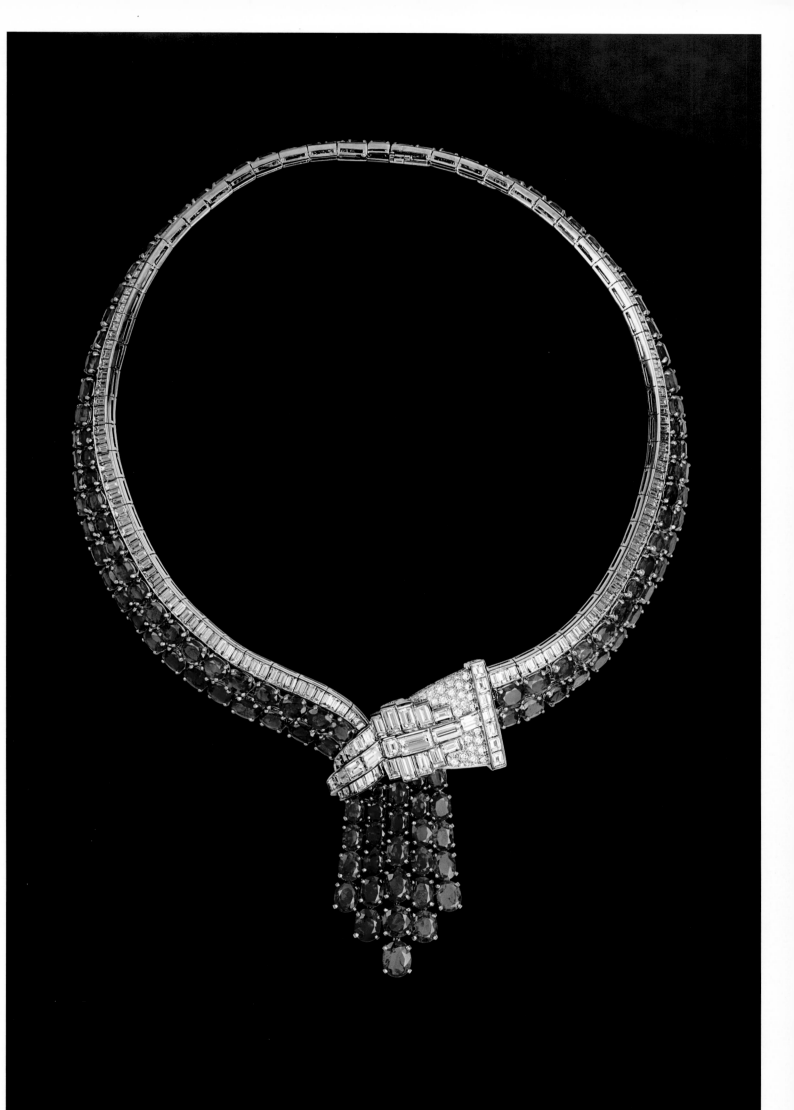

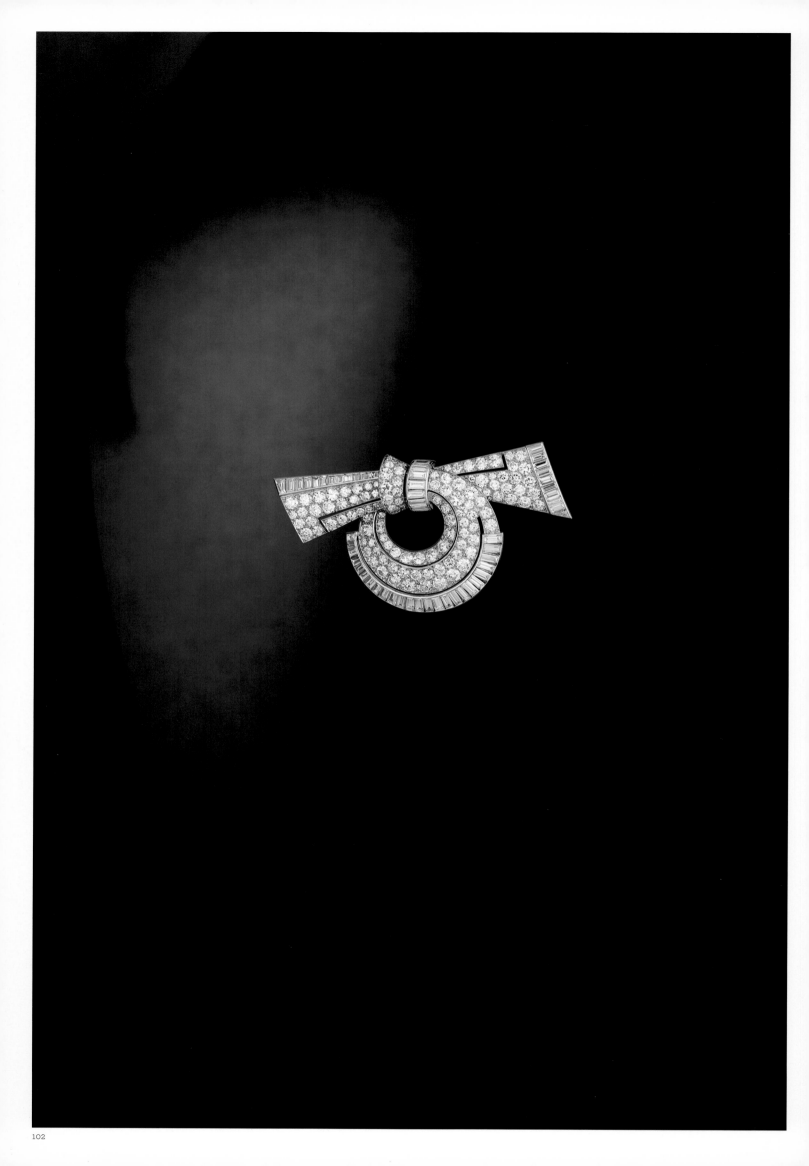

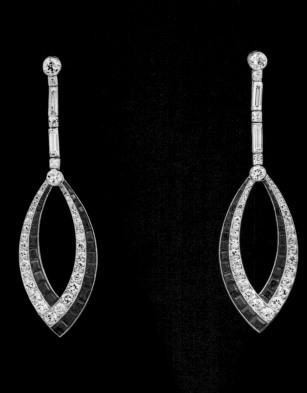

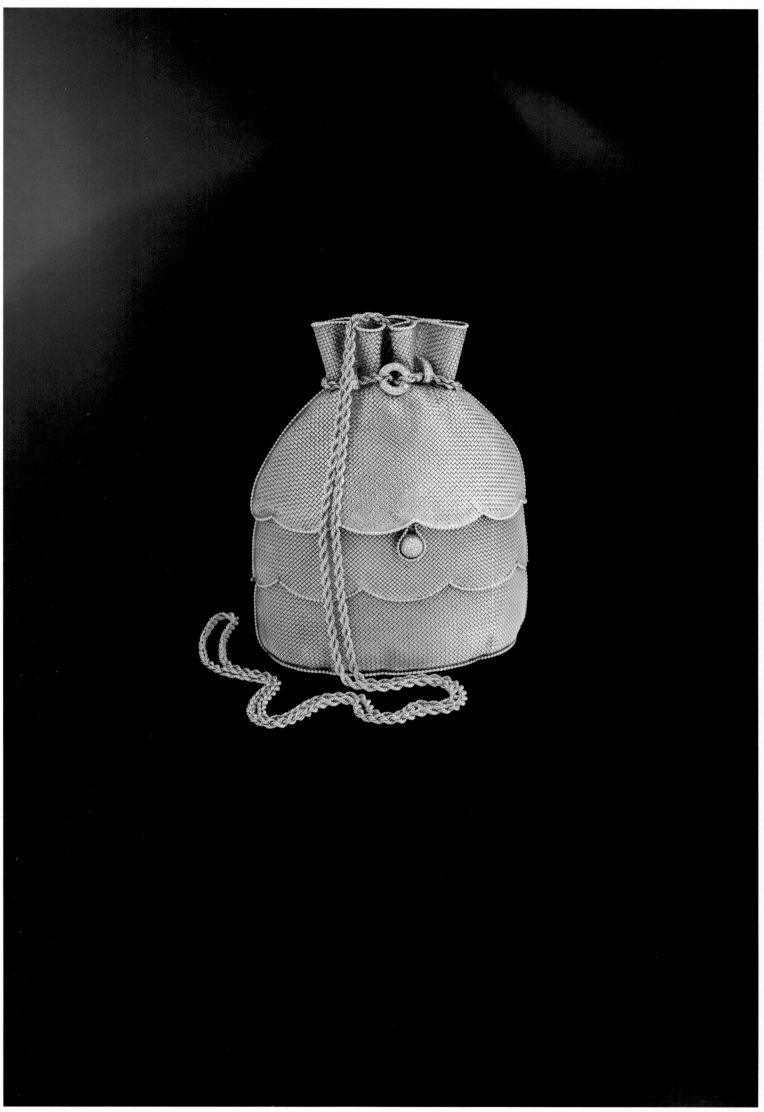

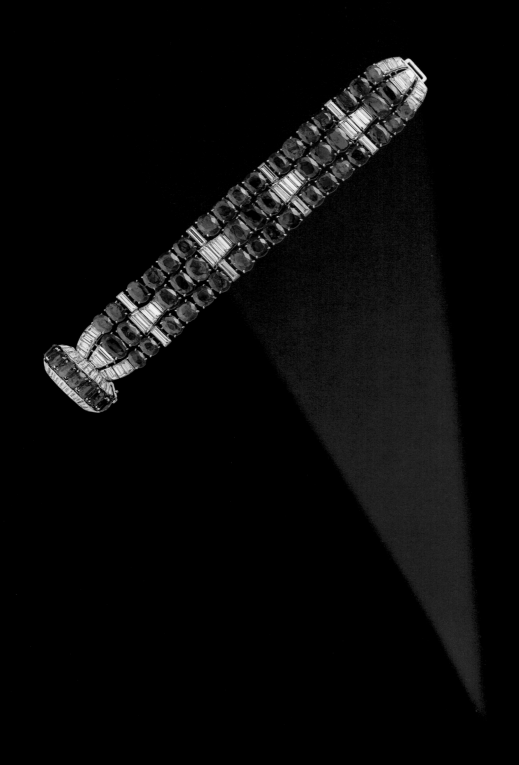

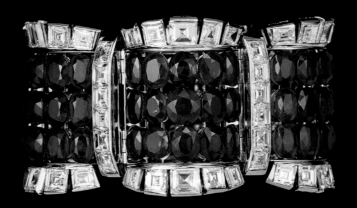

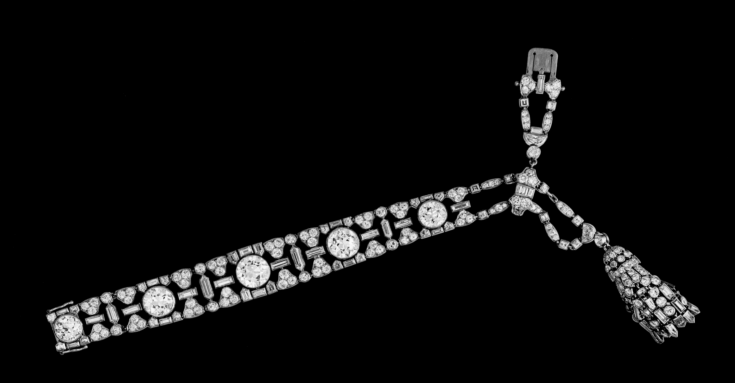

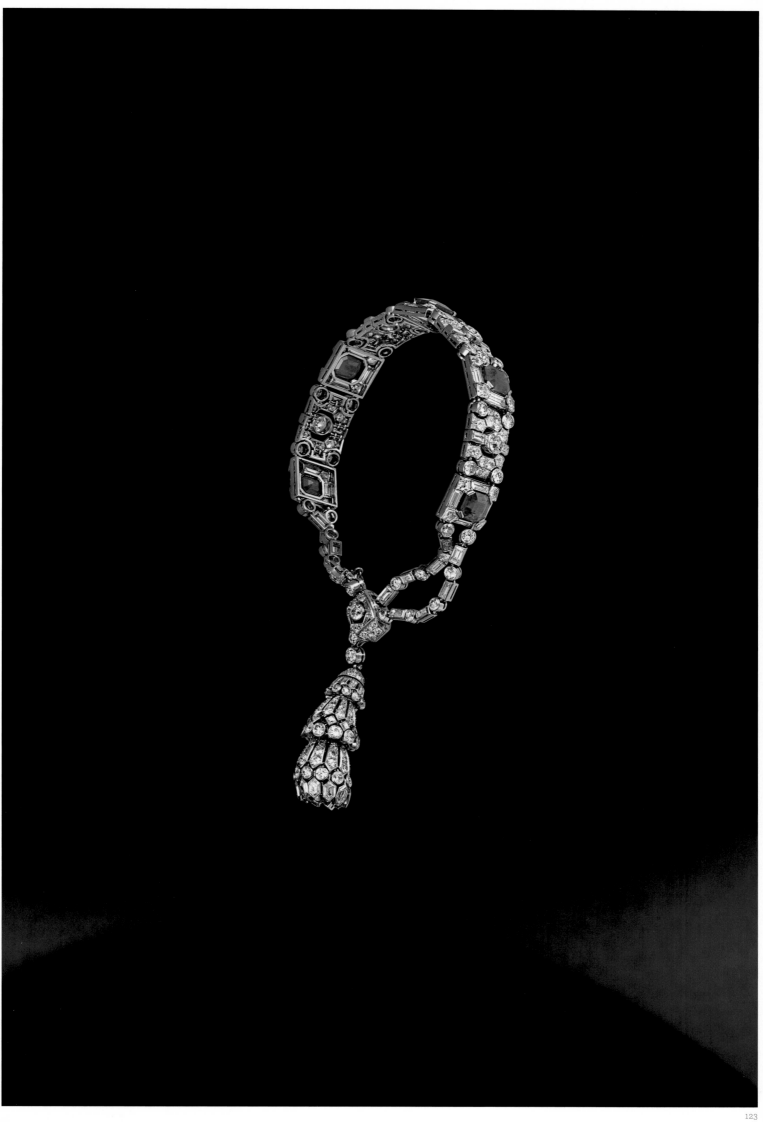

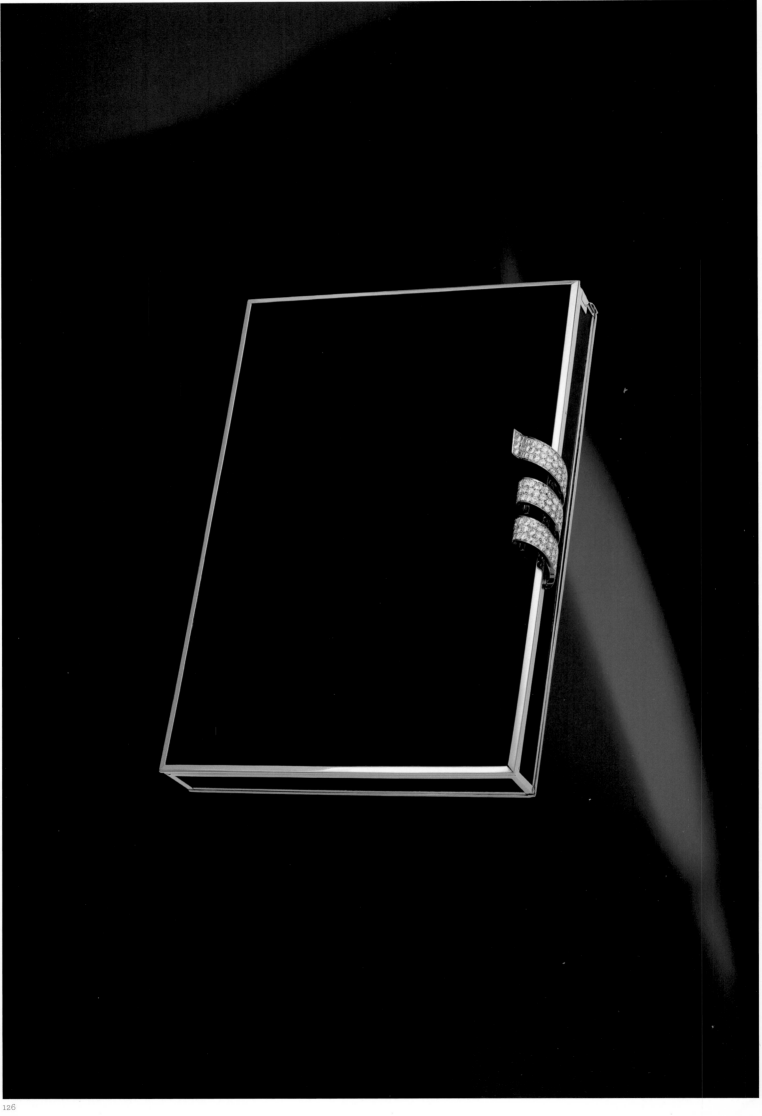

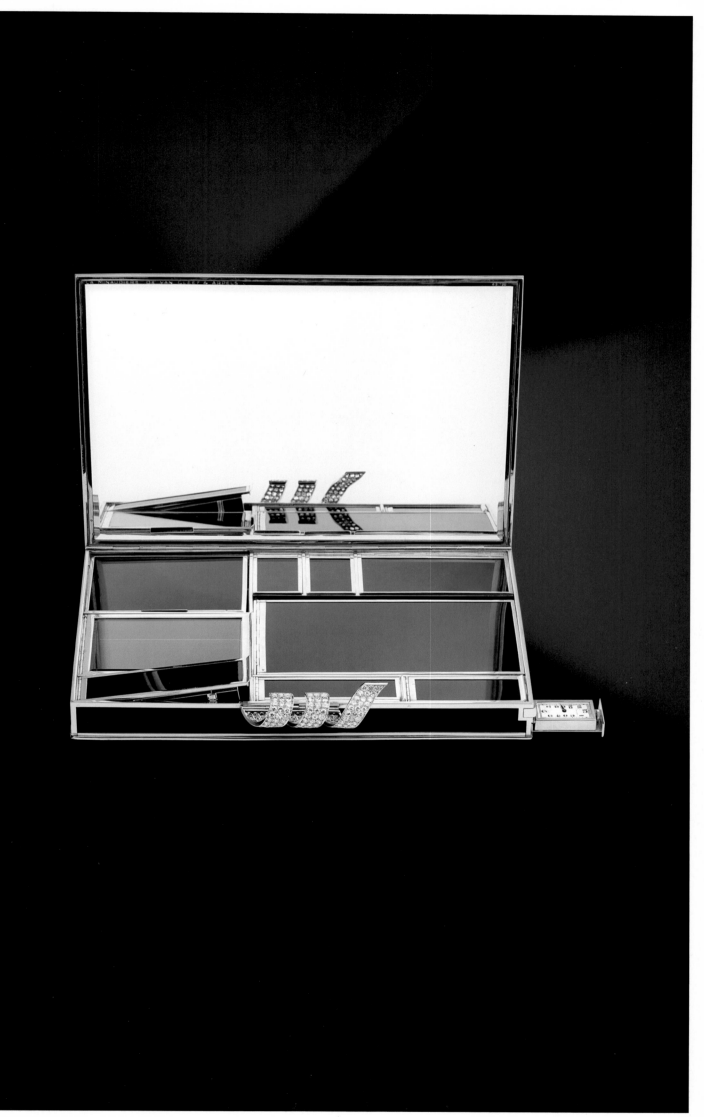

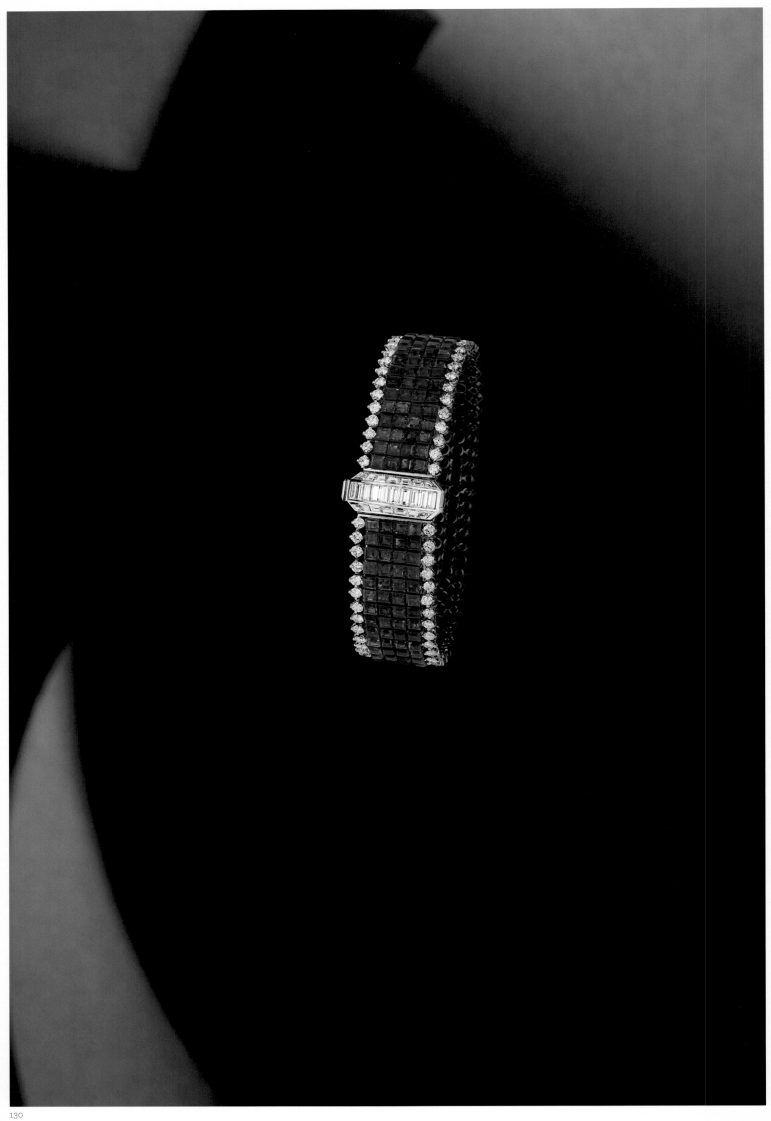

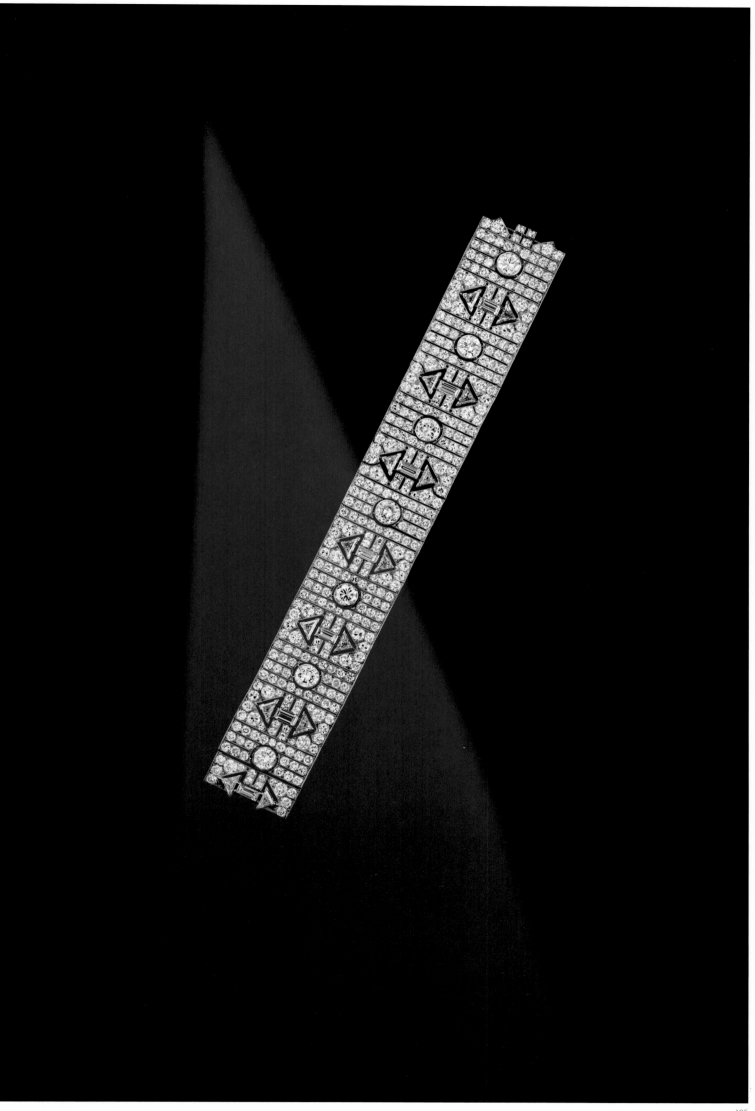

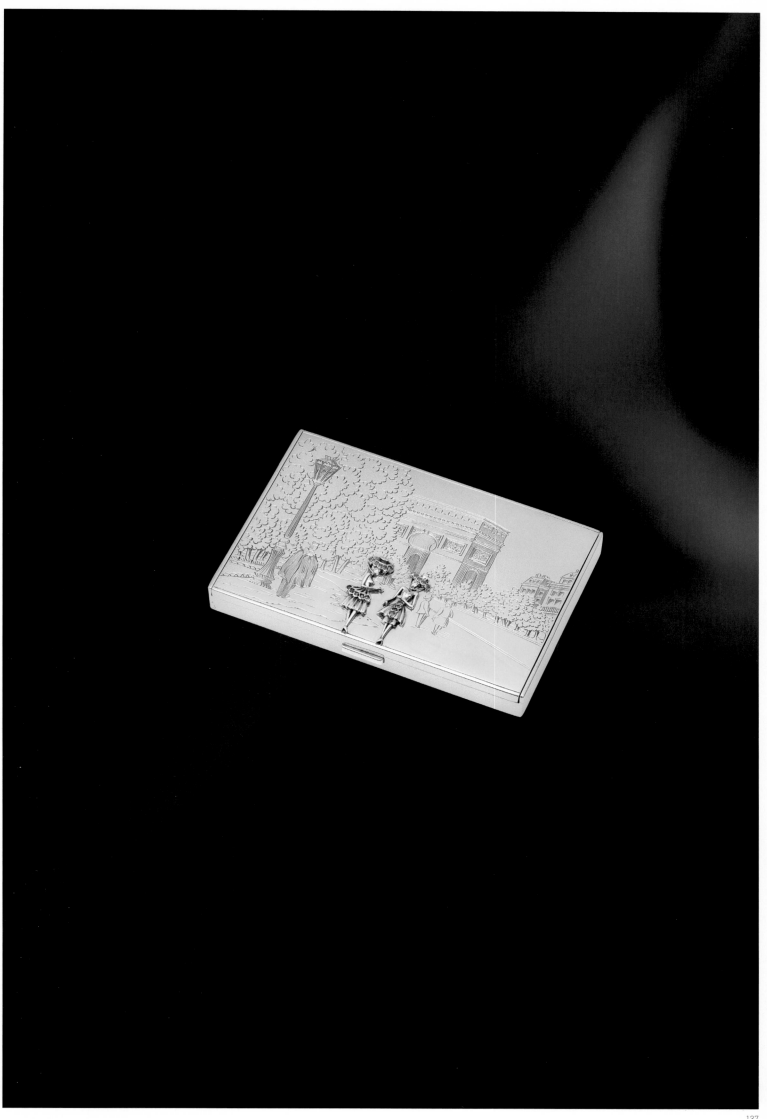

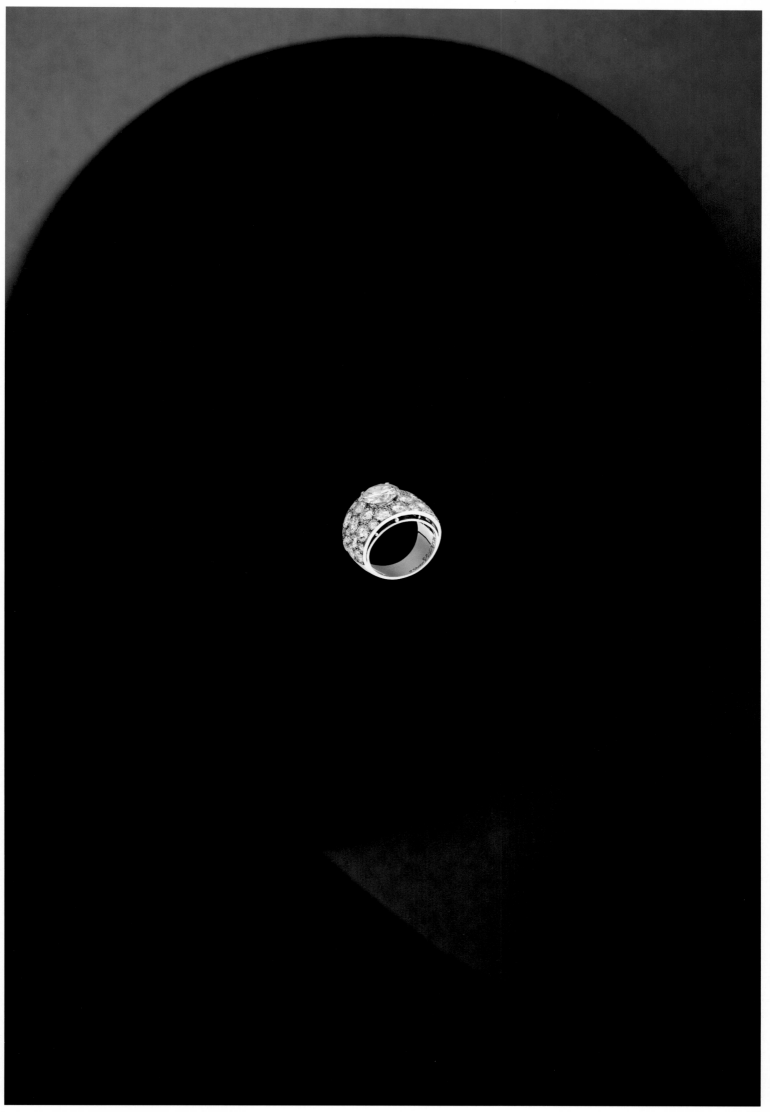

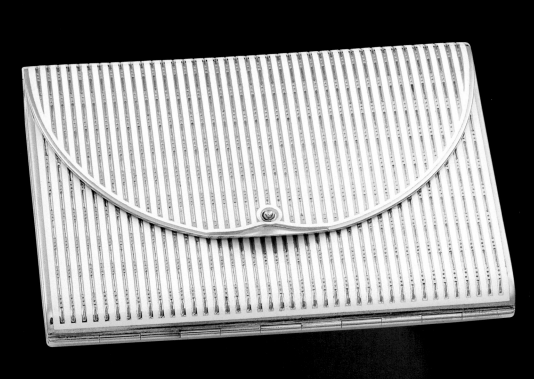

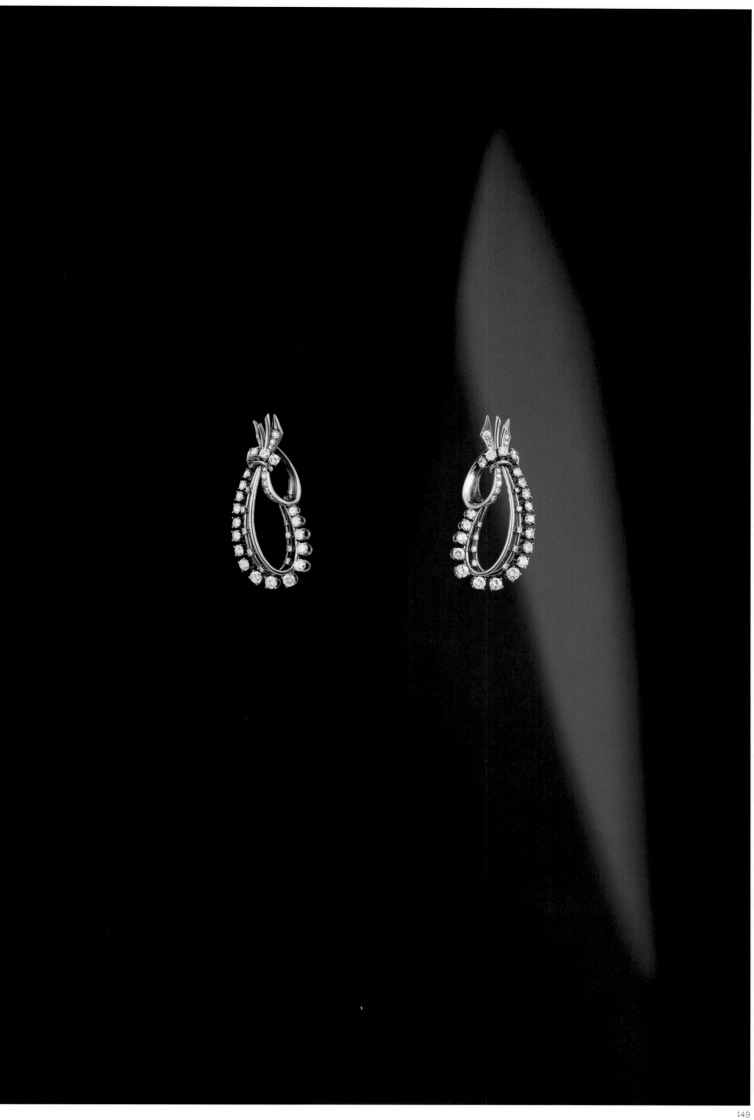

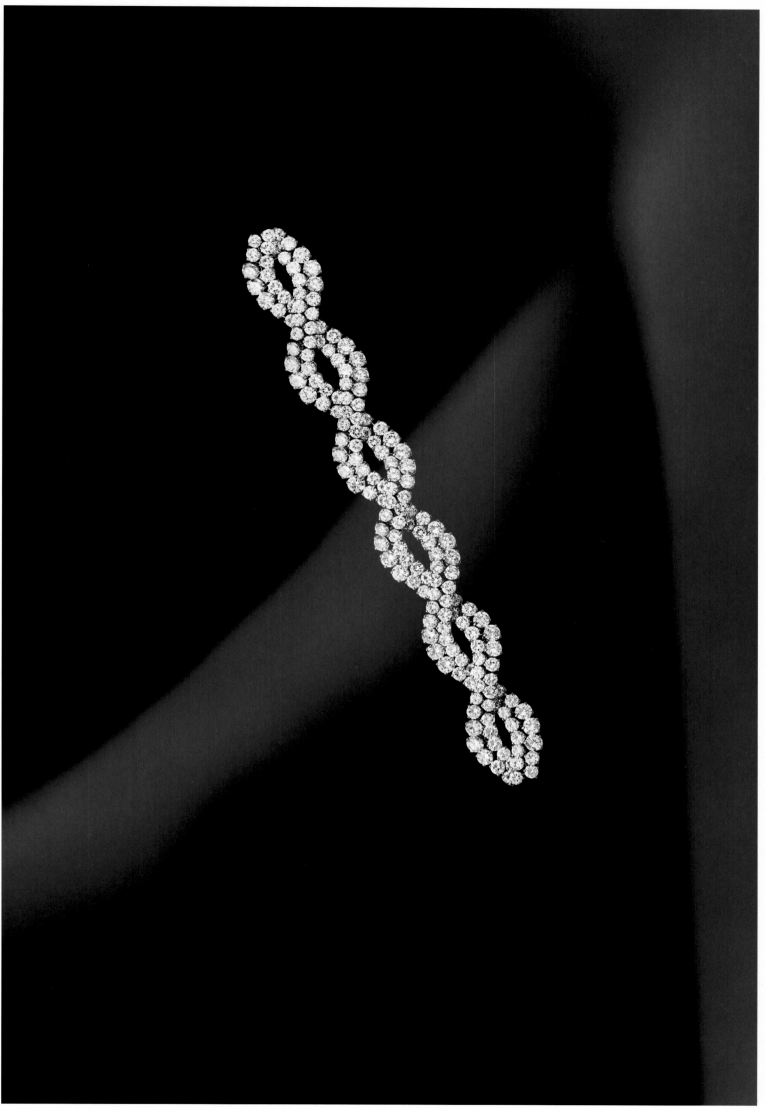

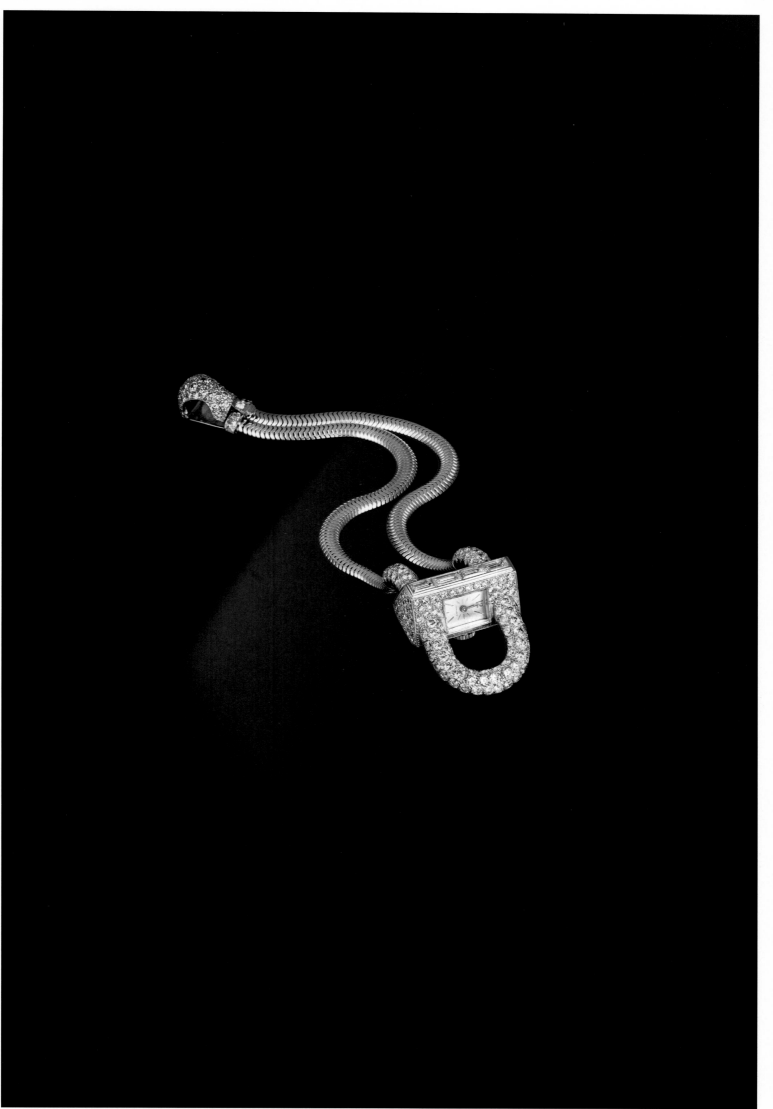

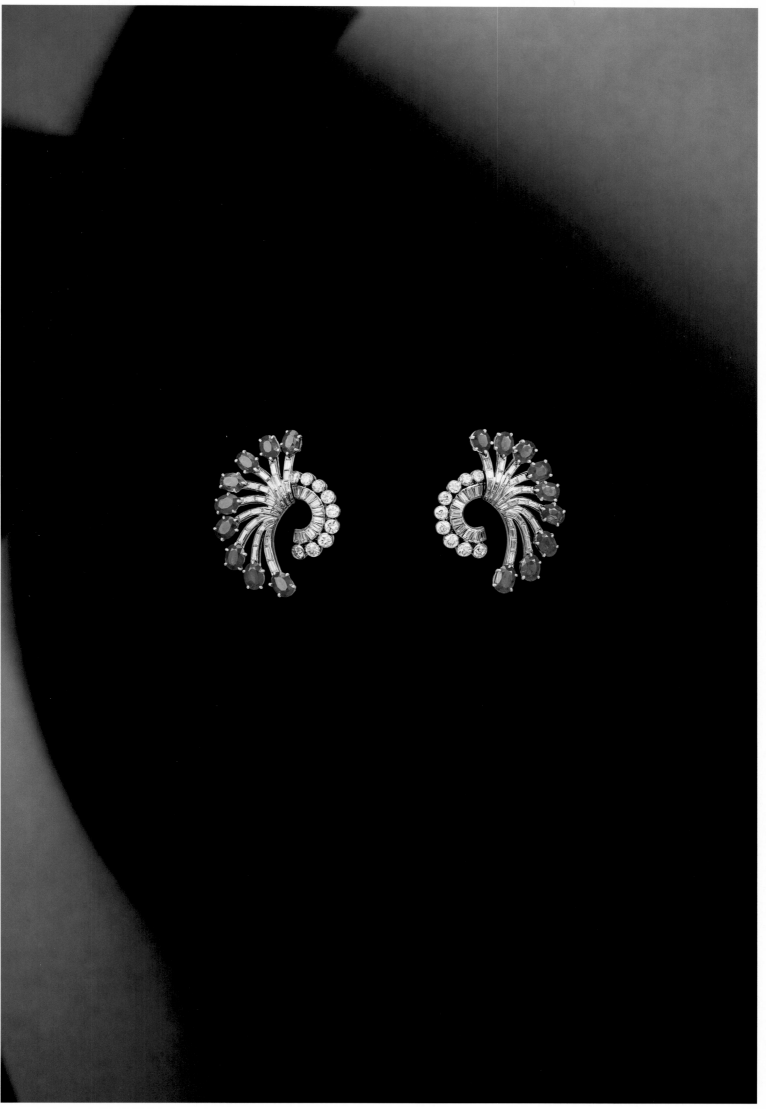

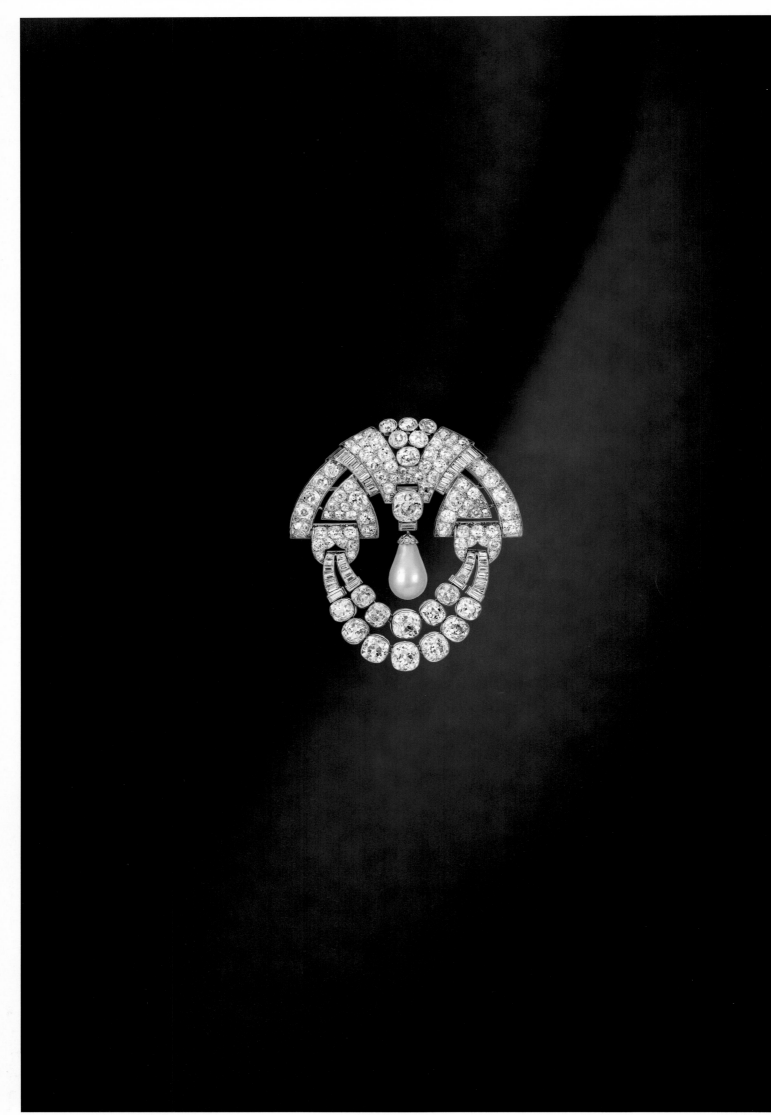

Spirit
of
Adventure

November 1922: archaeologist Howard Carter, heart pounding and candle in hand, finally penetrated Tutankhamen's tomb. The discovery hit the headlines in newspapers all over the planet. God bless the pharaoh! He was to set the imagination of our creators on fire. As the treasures of the young king were brought to light, our jewellery was adorned with ibises, sphinxes and crouching scribes... the thousand mysteries of Egypt.

Let us travel towards another wonder: India. India whose mines were overflowing with diamonds, India whose Maharajas staggered under the weight of the stones and pearls which covered them from head to toe, also adorning their horses and elephants. At the beginning of the 20th century, these princes came on pleasure trips to Europe, to London, of course, but also to Paris where they were welcomed with open arms. Our new friends brought with them suitcases overflowing with gems which they wanted to have reset according to our fashions. At that time, only the craftsmen of place Vendôme were able to master platinum work. In an exchange of courtesies, Indian jewellery in turn inspired the western muses. Its blue, red and green enamels inspired our creation of coloured compositions daringly blending sapphires, rubies and emeralds on the same piece. We borrowed and adapted India's styles. Van Cleef & Arpels therefore created a *vanki,* a bracelet worn above the elbow, featuring a shining Hindu god. Its style was reinterpreted, along with its gems that hang in clusters, cascades and drapes. A sumptuous illustration of the genre are the two flexible bracelets formed with geometric diamond motifs from which cabochon polished emeralds hang, which were to captivate Daisy Fellowes in 1926. Mrs Reginald Fellowes, the Singer sewing machine heiress, wore one on each arm: the quintessence of chic. No jealousy. On showy days she teamed them with a choker or diadem. More modestly, in 1947, "Radja" pendants began to spring up from our workshops in celebration of the independence Great Britain granted India that year. The next decade, Claude Arpels, following several interminable days of waiting in a dreamlike palace, successfully negotiated the purchase of the Maharajah de Rewa's treasure chest. It was an acquisition which reawakened the vogue for Indian products. Bearing witness to this was the splendid necklace set with 745 diamonds and 44 engraved emeralds, made for the princess Salimah Aga Khan.

The winds of the East blow from many places; they also reach us from Persia, by unexpected means: The Ballets Russes, in 1909, triumphed on the stage of the Théâtre du Châtelet in Paris. A year later, Diaghilev's company staged *Shéhérazade*. The public was dazzled by Léon Bakst's costumes with their shimmering colour contrasts. Was the designer not known as "the Gauguin of the Theatre?" The ever-extravagant couturier Paul Poiret organised a spectacular party, the "Thousand and Second Night". Colour shone forth at every turn. Where did the jewellery find such bold colours? From a palette of colored stones: coral, lapis-lazuli, jade, a mineral which is venerated in China and has been destined for Europe since the Sacking of the Summer Palace. Another event, the Boxer Rebellion, turned all cameras towards the Celestial Empire. Antiquarians set themselves up in Paris, specialists in Asian arts such as Loo who built a pagoda there! Exoticism invaded Art Deco. Chrysanthemum flowers blossomed on our vanity cases. Pot-bellied Buddhas were displayed on tables. The "Yellow Journey" financed by Citroën –followed by the "Black Journey"– added to the prevailing exoticism. This reached its climax in 1931 with the Colonial Exhibition which took place in the Bois de Vincennes in Paris. It drew 32 million visitors! On the Van Cleef &

Arpels stand they were won over by a golden set known as the "Chapeaux Chinois", "Chinese Hats".

The history of taste is merely one of comings and goings. The craze for luxury from the East resurfaced when the Shah of Iran, at the height of his power, launched extravagant festivities in Persepolis to commemorate 2,500 years of the Persian empire and assert its rediscovered grandeur. A peacock, inspired by a miniature, tail on display and adorned with precious stones, struts about on the lids of our powder compacts.

There are so many adventures linked to Van Cleef & Arpels! Like this miniature yellow gold and white enamel boat which rests on a block of jasper cut in such a way as to suggest a raging sea… The owner of the yacht *Varuna of New York*, Mr. Eugene Higghins, a rich, confident American sportsman, was so proud of his speedy craft that he commissioned a reproduction in around 1906. A marvel of progress, the ornament was electrified, allowing its owner to ring for the butler. It is wonderful to be well served! Another memorable order was this platinum vanity case, the diamond, sapphire and emerald decoration of which depicted a locomotive running out of steam and a car burning the tarmac. Babe Barnato, the president of Bentley who was passionate about motor racing, made a bet that he would reach Cannes from Paris more quickly than the Train Bleu. Bravo BB! This accessory commemorated his victory. Oh, the intoxicating speed that fired the Roaring Twenties! On the subject of intoxication, let us recall the amusing fashion which began in the 1930s for charm bracelets inspired by cocktails. On the gold and enamel model that we unveil here, each charm represented a vital ingredient for making a "Bronx": a bottle of vermouth, a decanter of gin, a shaker, an orange, an ice cube, the zest of a lemon… The time between the wars was extremely light-hearted. Twenty years of consumption and celebration without moderation.

Laurence MOUILLEFARINE

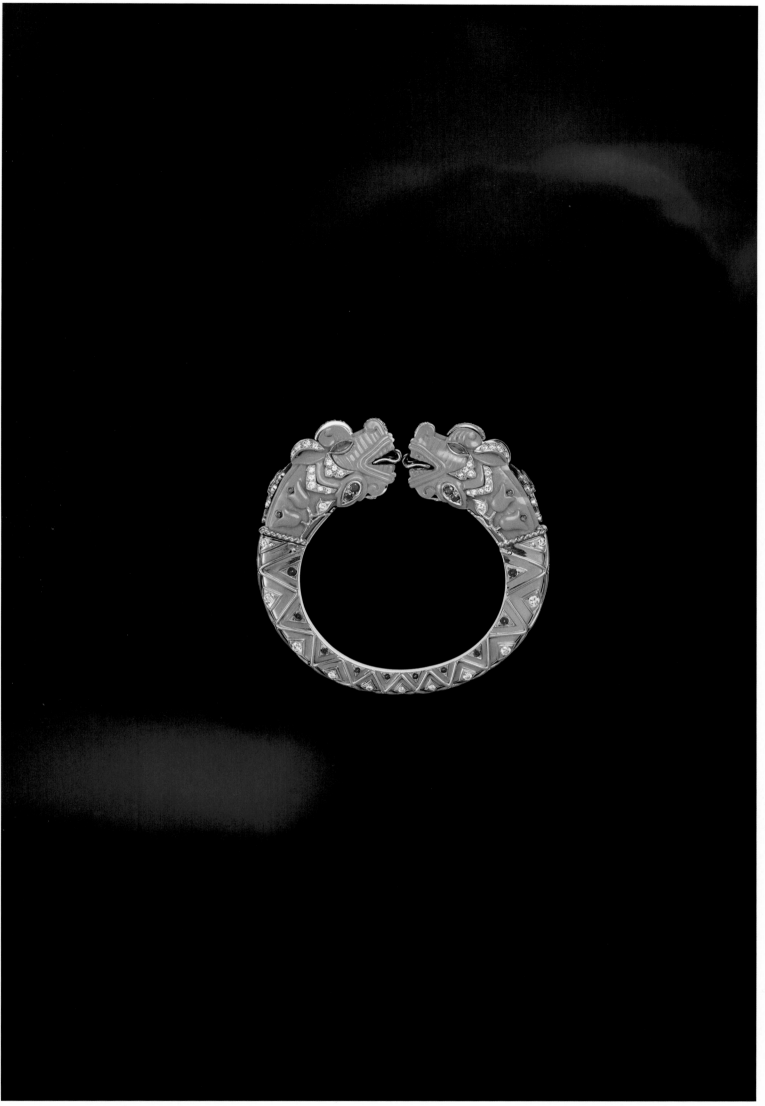

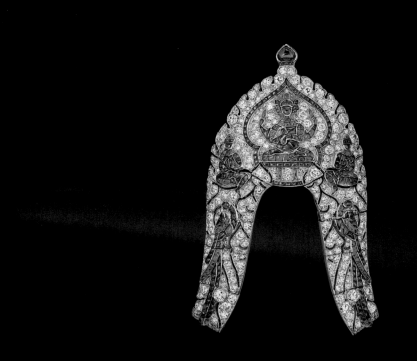

189

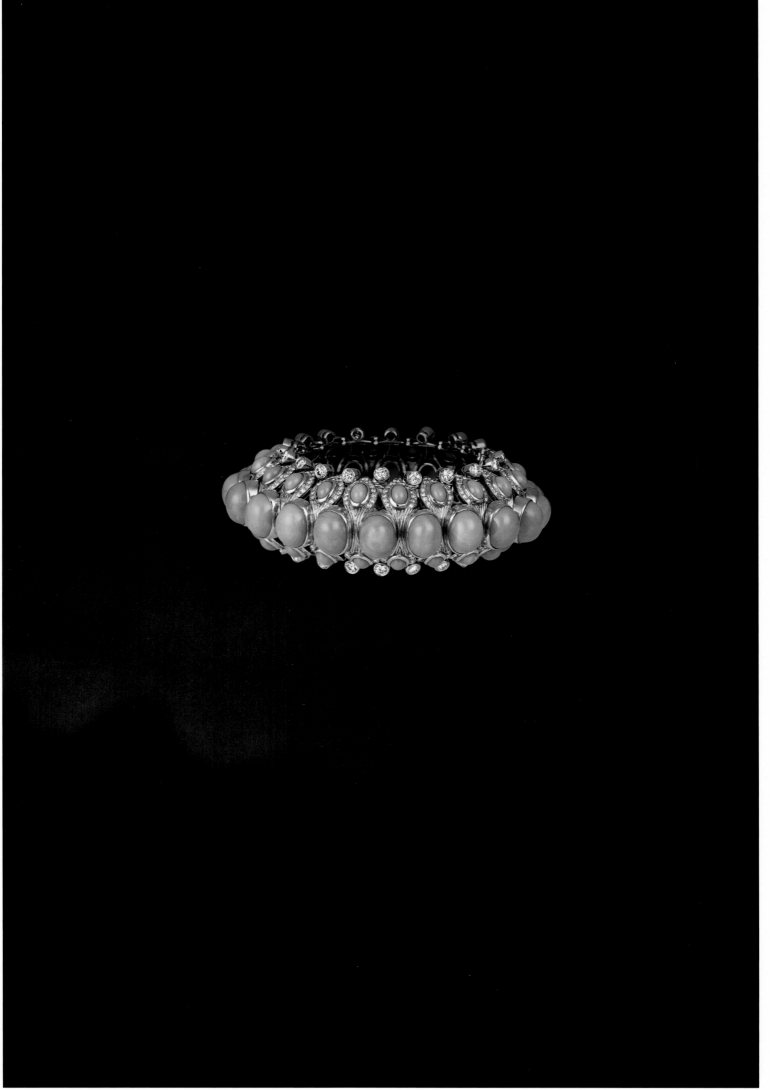

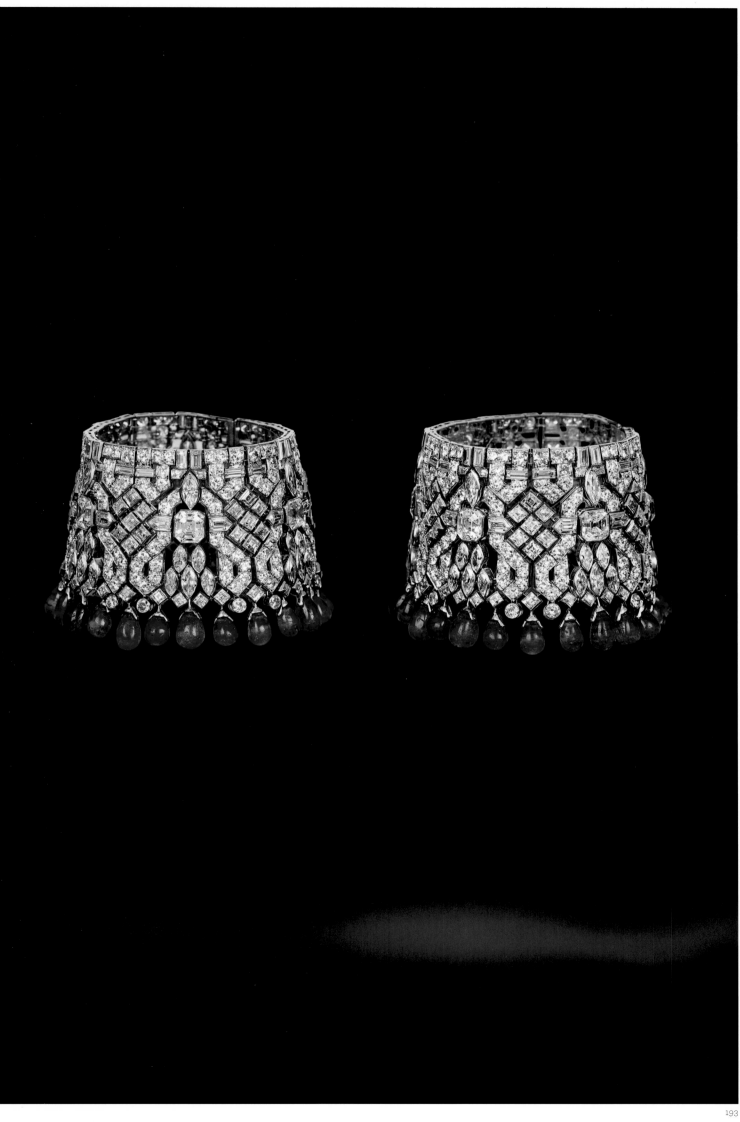

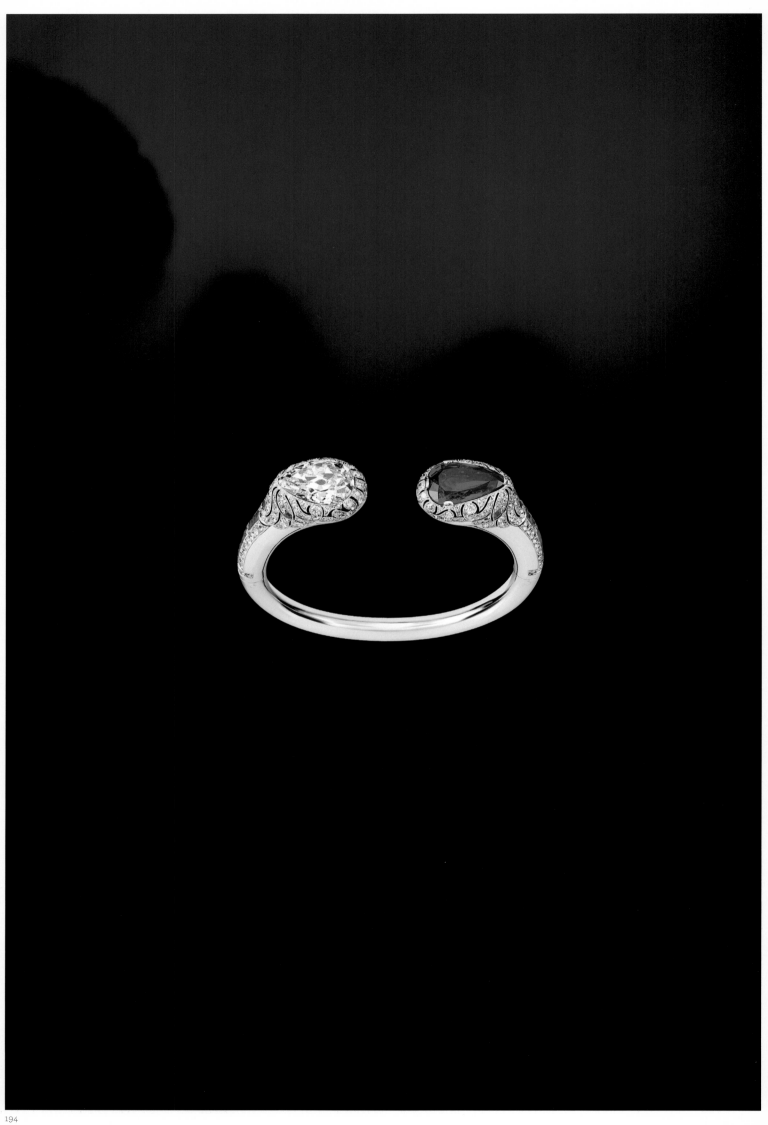

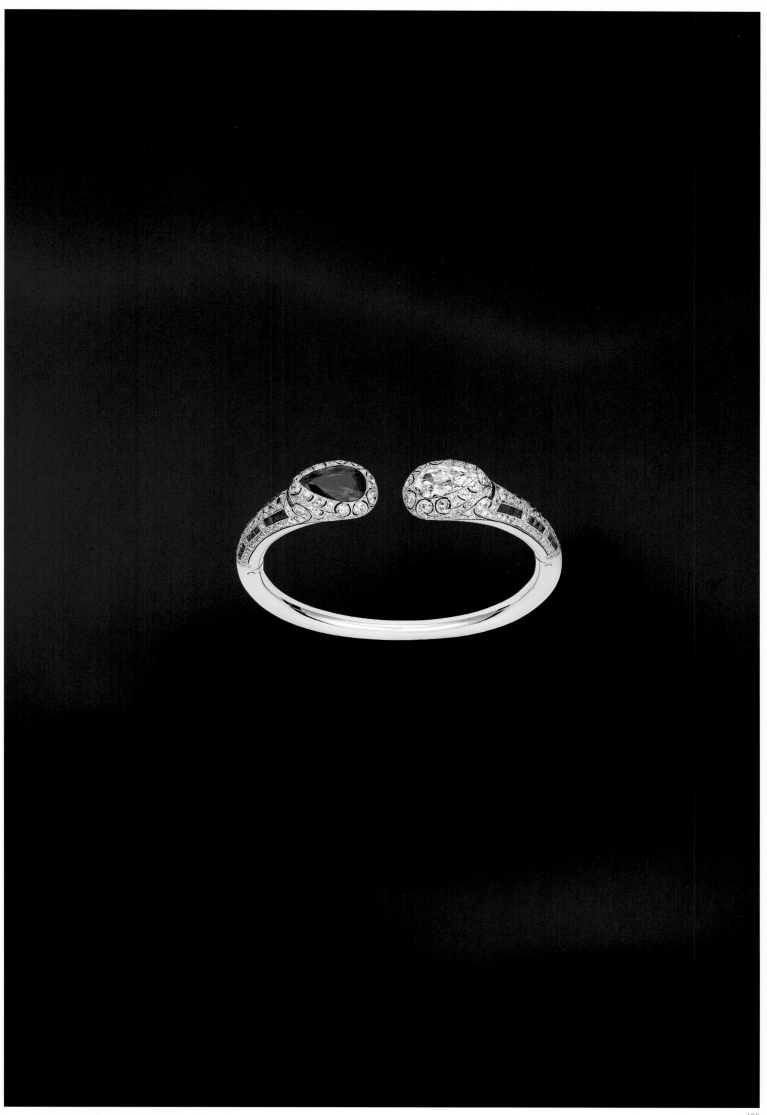

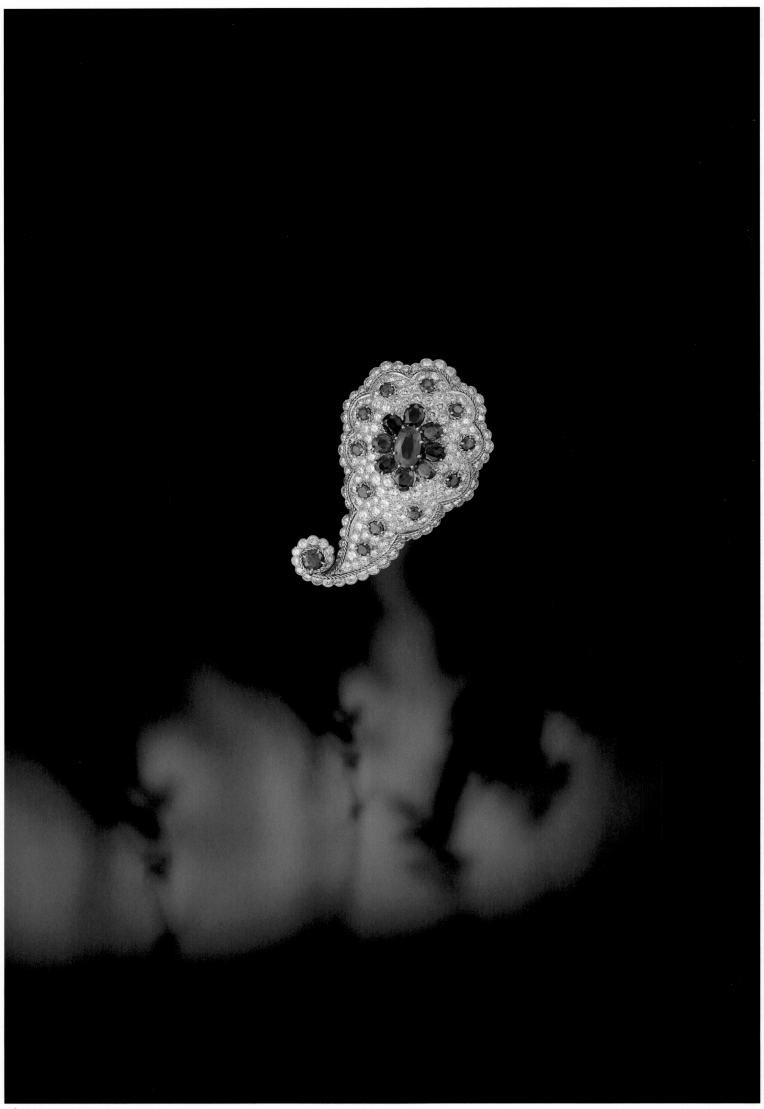

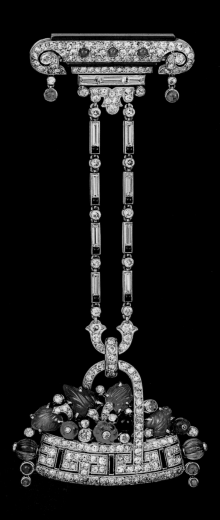

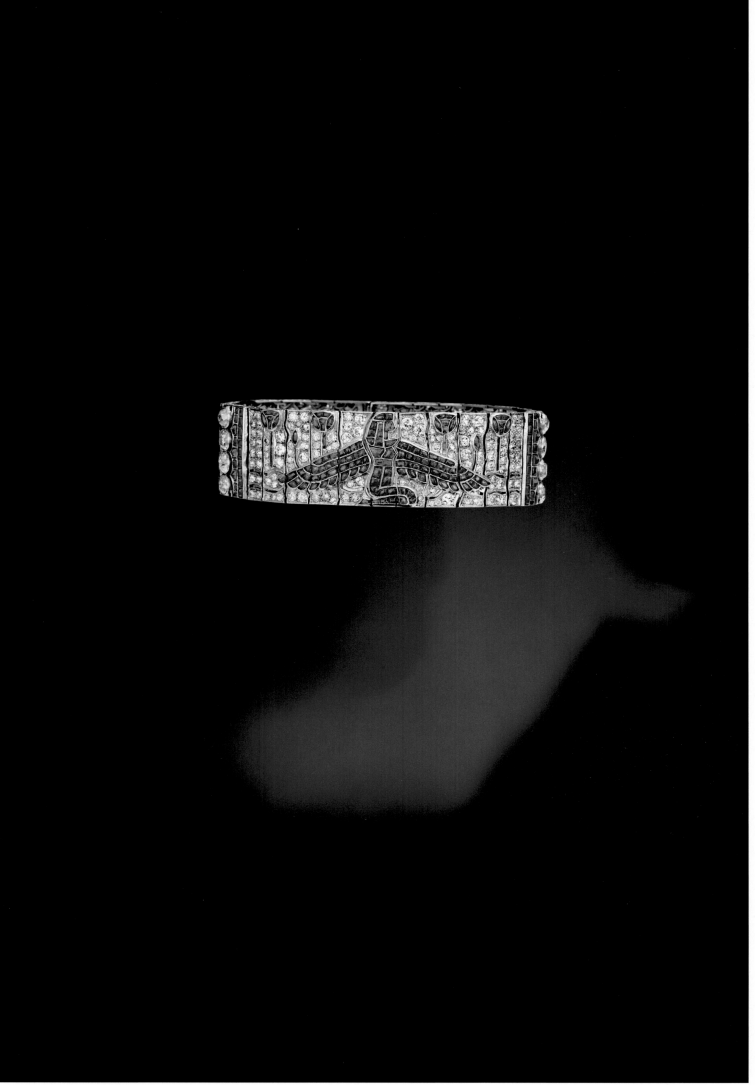

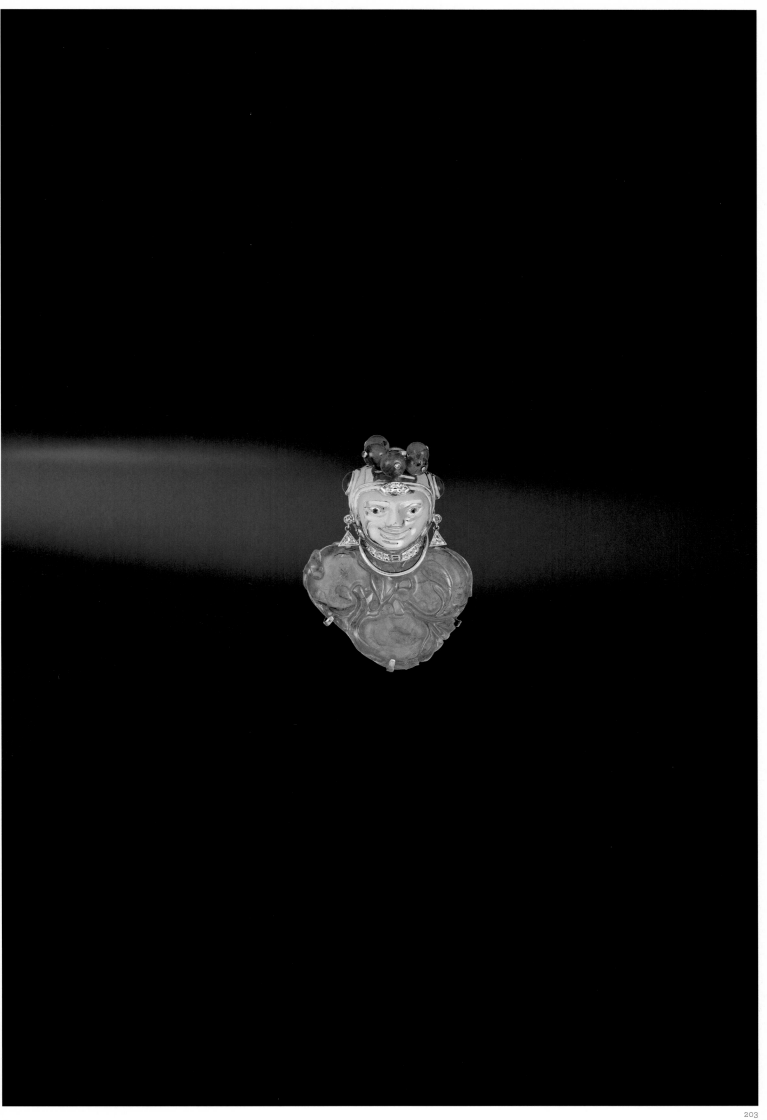

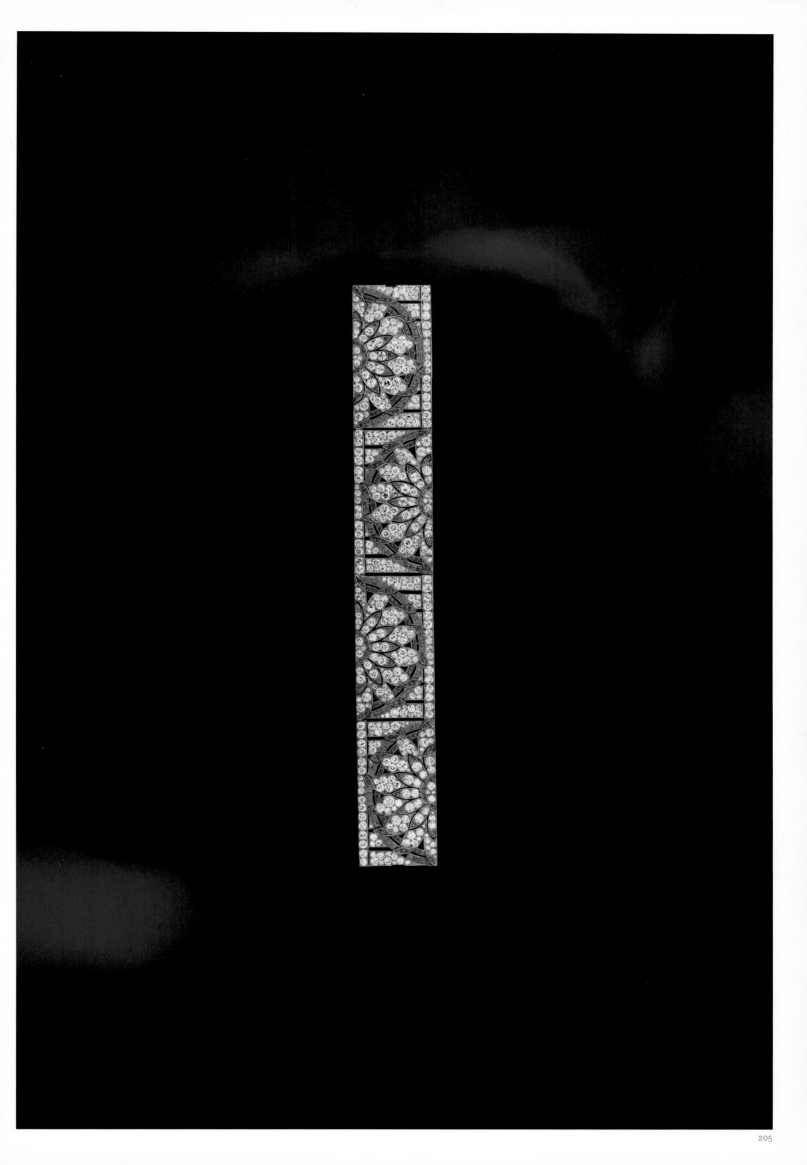

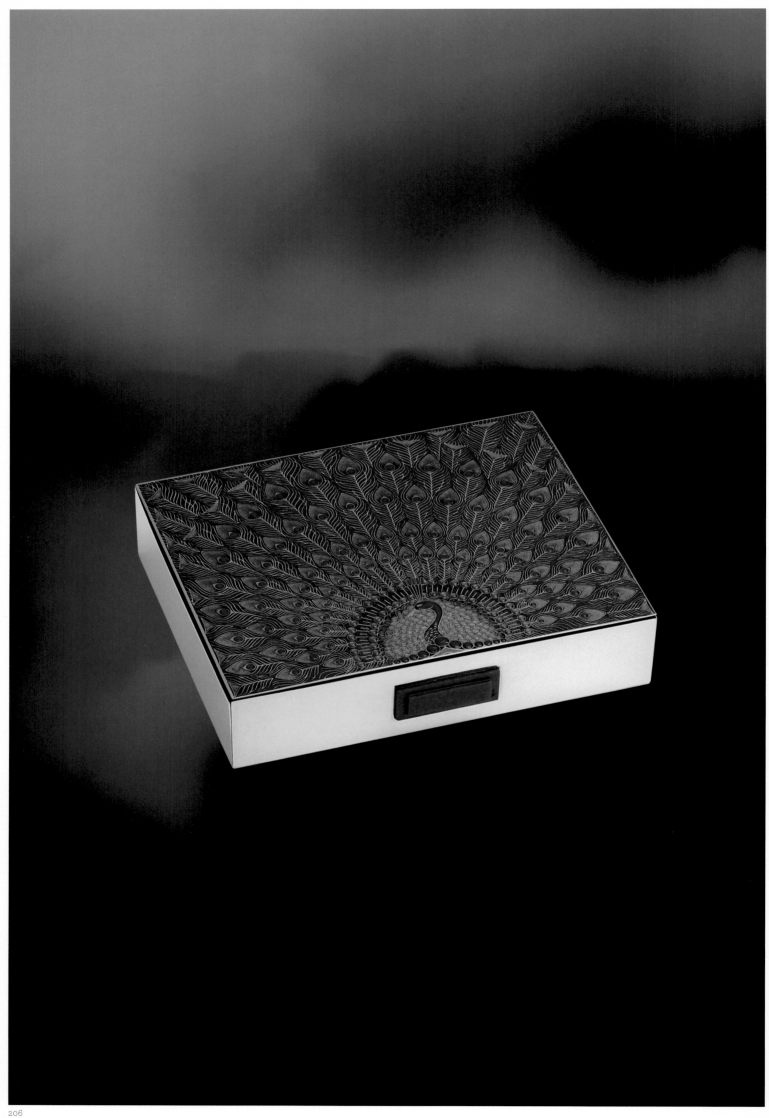

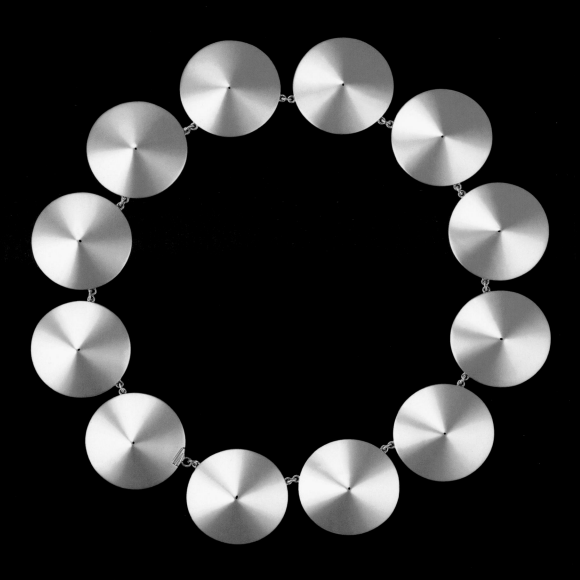

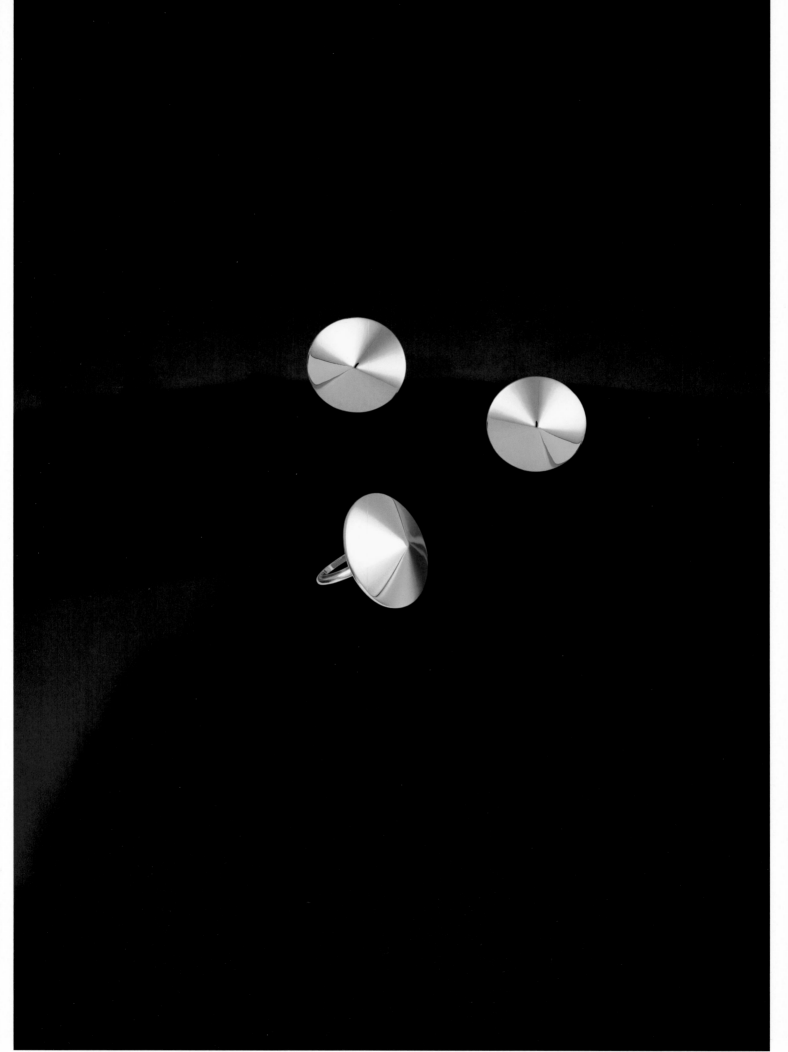

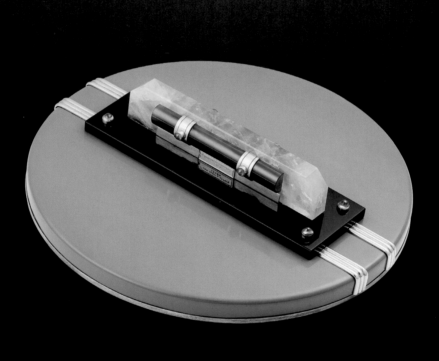

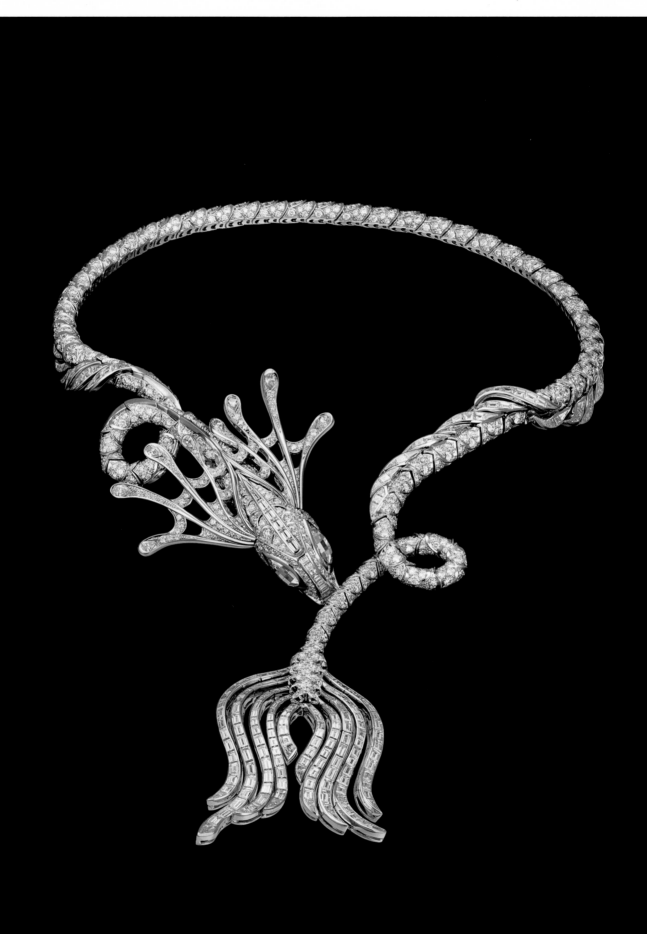

Incarnations

THEY SYMBOLISE a style, an era, the art of living... Barbara Hutton, Marlene Dietrich, Princess Soraya, Jackie Kennedy Onassis and Grace Kelly are legends who form part of the history of Van Cleef & Arpels.

It was one of those moments that count in the career of a jeweller. Pierre Arpels must have remembered it his whole life. Barbara Hutton (1912-1979), the billionaire with seven husbands, the woman who owned the most beautiful jewellery in the world, was staying in Paris. She had asked him to come to her hotel. A new order, perhaps? At least, he hoped so. Having arrived at Mrs Hutton's suite, he had been welcomed by his client's loyal butler: "Madam is a little unwell. She will receive you in her bedroom."

Having been shown to the room, Pierre Arpels witnessed an incredible spectacle: Barbara Hutton, lying down with her head resting on soft pillows bordered with lace, her head encircled by a halo of enormous diamonds, including a 54 carats pear-shaped gem. She loved the diamond diadem that he had delivered to her a few months earlier so much that she was wearing it in bed.

This absolutely true story symbolises an era in which elegance occasionally rubbed shoulders happily with extravagance. This refined world had its queens. They wrote their story in diamond, ruby, sapphire, emerald and pearl letters.

A yellowing document, which has been carefully preserved in the Van Cleef & Arpels archives, evokes this art of living: the inventory of Barbara Hutton's jewellery. Emeralds as big as matchboxes, one of which weighed 100 carats, rings, the largest set with a 44.58 carats navette diamond, tens of pairs of earrings, a ruby necklace which could be worn as a diadem, three necklaces with several rows of natural pearls, each the size of a hazelnut.

Upon her death in 1976, Barbara, who had lost her fortune, left her heirs just $4000, but her jewellery collection remained intact. She had preserved it until her very last breath.

One of the flagship items of this exhibition is the amazing ruby and diamond bracelet ordered in 1973 by one of Hollywood's greatest stars, Marlene Dietrich (1901-1992). "Invented" by Paramount at the beginning of the 1930s as a rival to Greta Garbo, the Swedish star of MGM, Dietrich was an excessive personality in every way.

At that time, she was one of the symbols of femininity, despite dressing like a man. In Hollywood, she lived with her husband, Rudi, and daughter, Maria. Both called her "Mutti", German for "Mom", but her love life was a tornado involving celebrities of both genders. At one famous soirée, she amused herself by distributing carnations among the men present: red for old lovers and white for her suitors.

The director Joseph von Sternberg immortalised her glamour in a series of seven films made between 1930 and 1935. *The Blue Angel* and *Shanghai Express* are the best-known of these. On-screen, he transformed Marlene in to an ultra-sophisticated goddess. Clever lighting was used to hollow out her cheeks. Before each take, a make-up artist re-applied a golden line on the bridge of her nose to reduce its curved appearance. For her costumes, the star demanded real feathers, real fur and of course real jewellery.

Upon her request, Louis Arpels created a bracelet, the shape of which was reminiscent of certain exotic flowers which use their beauty to attract their prey before devouring them. This is the perfect example of what a unique order can be, personalised in the extreme, on the border between a piece of jewellery and a work of art.

Marlene wore it in *Stage Fright*, filmed in 1950 under the direction of Hitchcock. It was sold at auction at Sotheby's in New York a few months after her death in 1992 for $900,000.

"Tragic queens" also have their place in the gallery of Van Cleef & Arpels icons. The best known of these is Soraya Esfandiari Bakthiari (1932-2001). Her destiny was played out between two dates: February 12, 1951 and February 13, 1958.

The first is that of her marriage to the Shah of Iran. Initially planned for the end of 1950, the ceremony was postponed by several weeks. Soraya, then aged 18, had been taken ill with typhoid. She was confined to her bed for over a month. Every day her fiancé brought her a gift: a pair of "Mimosas" clips, assorted earrings, a "Corde" necklace and a diamond bracelet, the central motif of which concealed a miniature watch. Some of these pieces are exhibited here.

The second date was the day on which she left Iran her marriage having been dissolved due to her inability to have children. She moved to Rome, then Munich and finally Paris where she died on October 25, 2001, having lived for 44 years after her great love story.

Her jewellery collection was dispersed a few months later. It included twenty Van Cleef & Arpels pieces. Among the most remarkable of them were two rings. The first, dating from 1951, was set with a 6.23 carats canary diamond. The second, decorated with a 7.89 carats diamond, had been purchased by the Shah at the end of the year 1957. A few weeks later, these two stones were to frame the tragic fairy tale of the "sad-eyed princess."

If Soraya was crushed by her destiny, Jacqueline Bouvier Kennedy Onassis (1929-1994) was always forced to stand up to it. The world discovered her on November 22, 1963, the day on which her husband, John Fitzgerald Kennedy, 35th President of the United States, was assassinated in Dallas. It was one of the most famous images in the history of the press.

Five years later, the most famous widow in the world remarried. On October 20, 1968, on the Greek island of Skorpios, Jackie exchanged the Kennedy name which was such a burden for that of the Greek billionaire Aristote Onassis. All the gifts that she received from her new husband came from Van Cleef & Arpels' New York boutique. The most impressive is a set comprising a necklace, ring and earrings set with diamonds and large emerald and ruby cabochons. Onassis then presented Jackie with other Van Cleef & Arpels sets. They were adorned with rubies, emeralds and diamonds.

This second union also ended sadly. When Onassis died in 1975, the couple was already separated. Jackie then returned to New York where she became an editor. Her two marriages, two widowhoods and unrivalled style made her a veritable legend. She remained as such until her death in 1994. Still today, the "Jackie O" look remains a classic: round, slightly convex sunglasses, a small pill box hat, a pastel suit... And a few elegant, discreet pieces of jewellery.

The place of honour in this portrait gallery goes to the woman who experienced not one, but two fairy tales. It was 53 years ago, on April 12, 1956...

That day, there were thousands of people crammed on the quay of the small port of Monaco, staring at the boat as it slowly approached. 5000 Monegasques and over 2000 journalists from all over the world had come to attend an event which at that time seemed highly implausible: the marriage of the least well-known prince of Gotha to the most famous star of Hollywood.

Two silhouettes appeared on the bow of the *Deo Juvante*, the Prince's yacht. A confident man, as befits a prince returning to his land. An elegant, yet discreet woman in her black silk coat, her eyes concealed under the curved edges of her wide-brimmed white organdie hat.

Their story travelled the world. They had met in France a year earlier on the occasion of the Cannes festival. At the age of twenty-six, Grace Kelly (1929-1982) was already a global star. She had just won her first Oscar for her role in *The Country Girl*. In five years, she managed to film four masterpieces: *High Noon, Dial M for Murder, Rear Window* and *Mogambo*. Prince Rainier of Monaco was 32 years old. He had reigned since 1949 over one of the smallest states in the world.

Nobody suspected their love at first sight. And on January 5, 1956, when their engagement was announced from the Kelly family residence in Philadelphia, the whole world awoke in a state of shock. It was at that moment that Van Cleef & Arpels became part of their legend.

A few days after the engagement, the prince went to the New York boutique to choose a "souvenir" for his fiancée. Diamonds? Coloured stones? He hesitated… and Louis Arpels finally succeeded in convincing him. Pearls, better than any other gem, would suit Miss Kelly's delicate beauty. The set comprised a three-row necklace and bracelet, embellished with platinum and diamond motifs, a ring and a pair of earrings.

Grace wore this jewellery for the first time on their honeymoon, during a stopover on the island of Majorca. It would accompany her throughout her life, like the other jewellery that Van Cleef & Arpels would create for her. A set of diamonds, the motifs of which, in the form of a swan, paid homage to her last role in the film entitled *The Swan*. Earrings and a bracelet set with diamonds. Long gold necklaces set with colored stones, including an emblematic model from the Alhambra collection. A sapphire and diamond clip which she is wearing in Ricardo Maccaron's large official portrait which is today preserved at the Prince of Monaco's palace.

And then, there were the sets lent to her from the jewellery collections for one evening on the occasion of exceptional events. These include the diamond diadem that she wore on the eve of the wedding of Princess Caroline, the Prince and Princess of Monaco's eldest daughter. That evening, Grace was 49 years old. She was still fabulously beautiful. She had retained the incredible charisma that would make Marc Bohan, Dior stylist, remark, "She had an extraordinary aura. As soon as she appeared anywhere, she took people's breath away. It is inexplicable."

The dual fairy tale of Grace Kelly, HSH the Princess of Monaco, ended prematurely in 1982 when she was killed in a car accident. But like Barbara Hutton, Marlene Dietrich, Soraya and Jackie O, she has remained a legend. During our modern era, which often has difficulty in expressing an identity, these five women still represent a timeless fundamental value which goes beyond fleeting fashions, a value dear to Van Cleef & Arpels: elegance.

Vincent MEYLAN

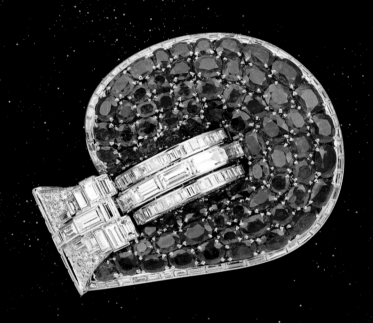

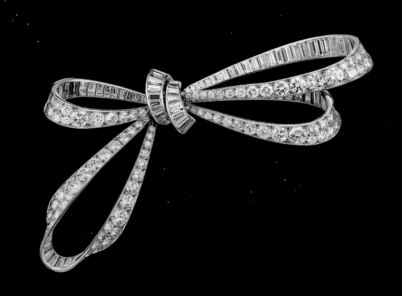

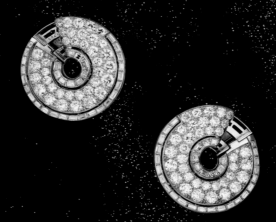

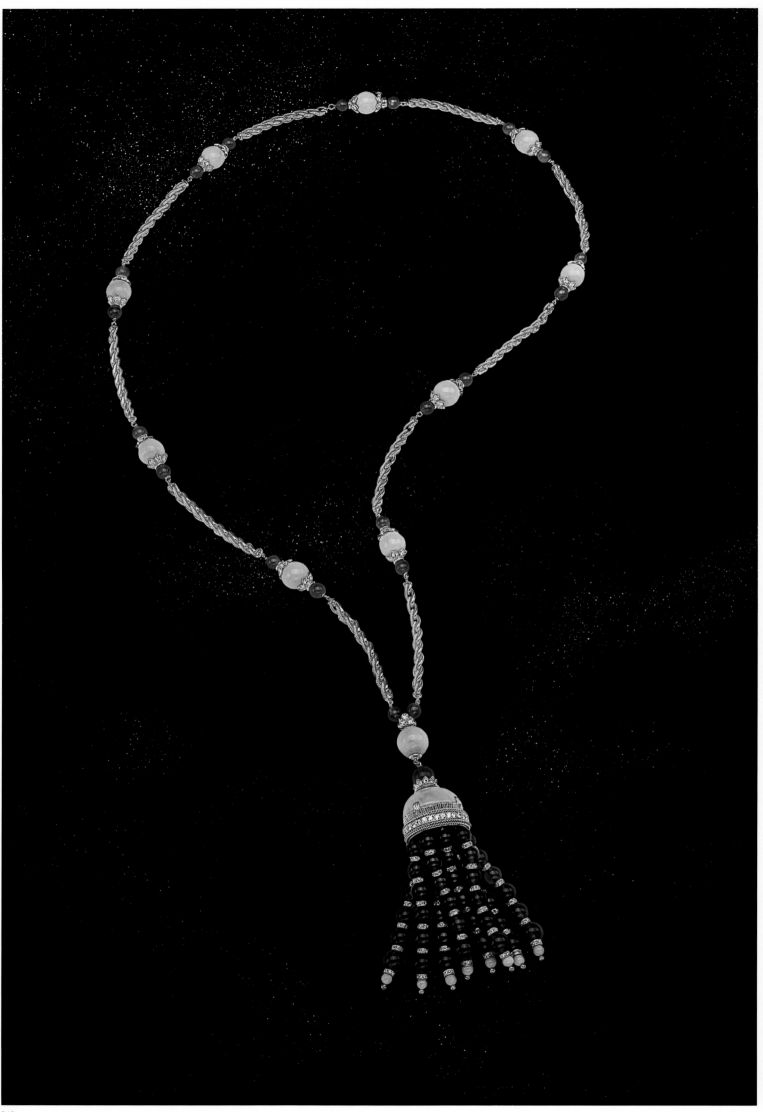

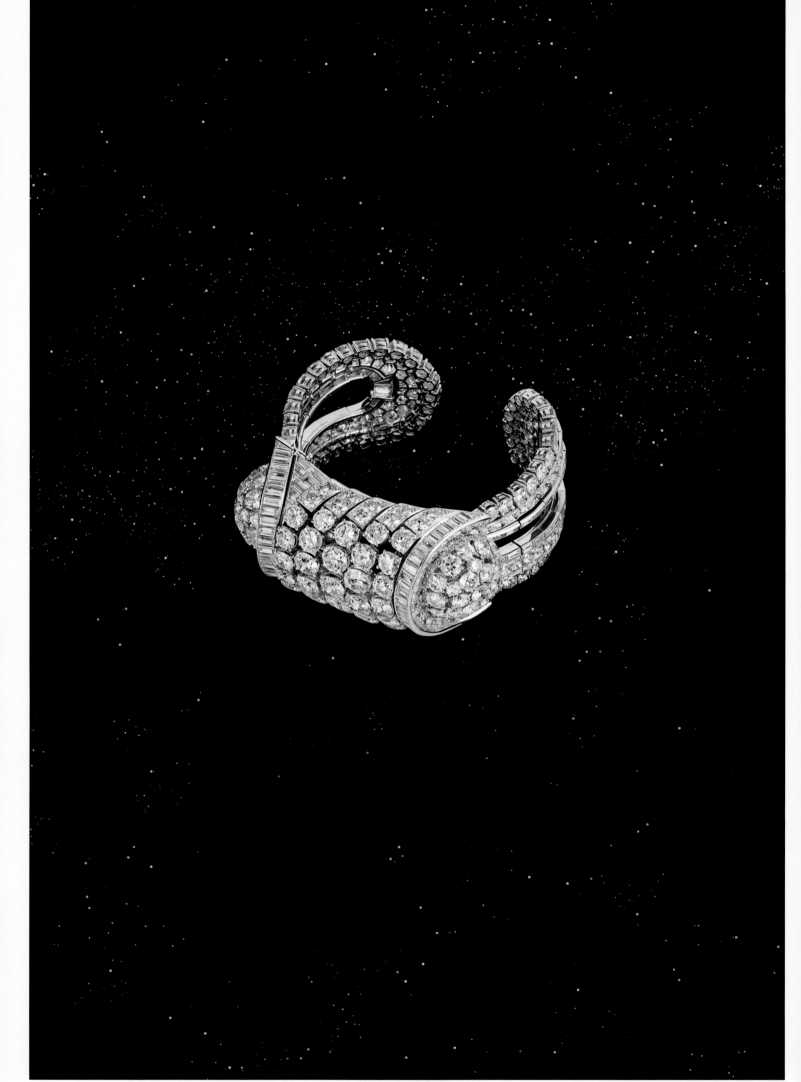

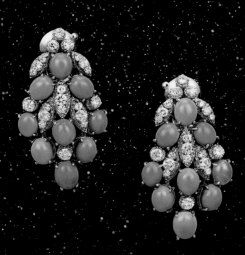

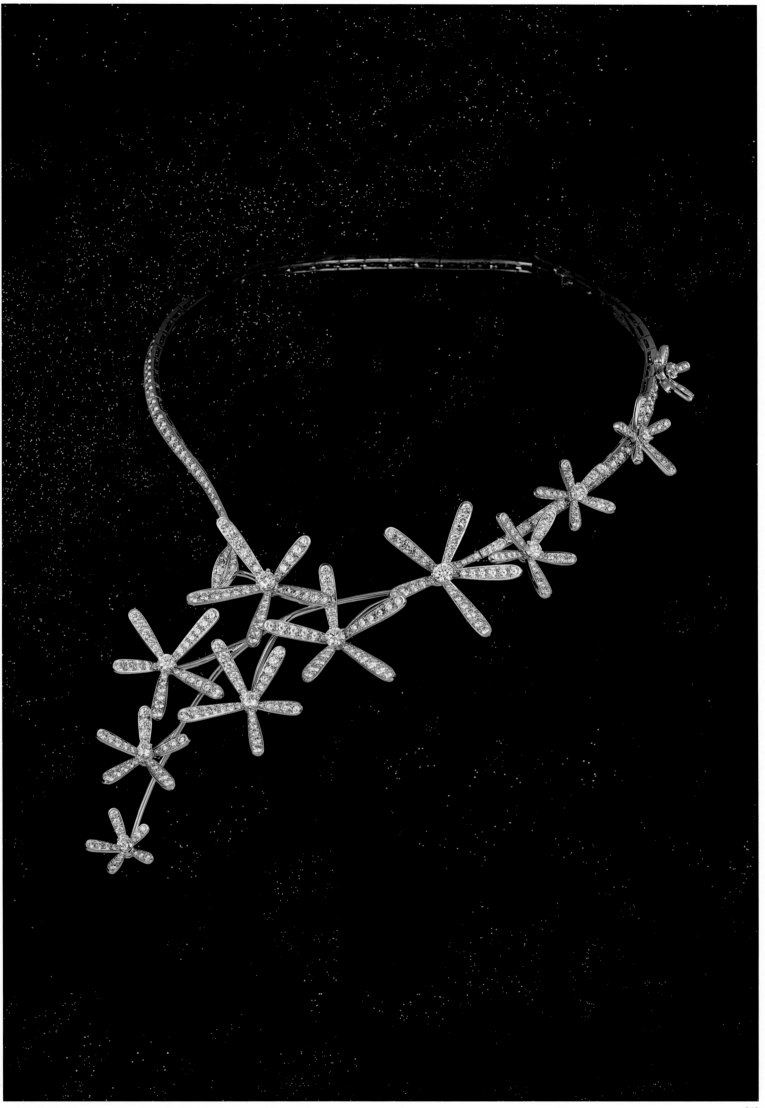

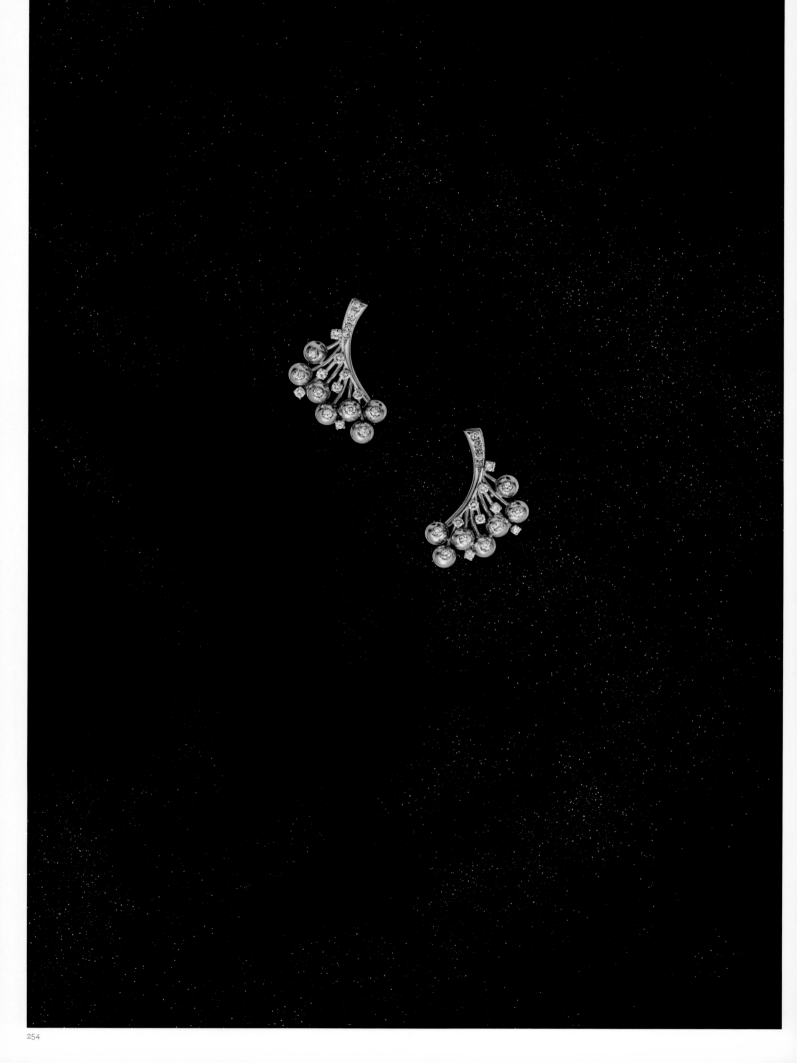

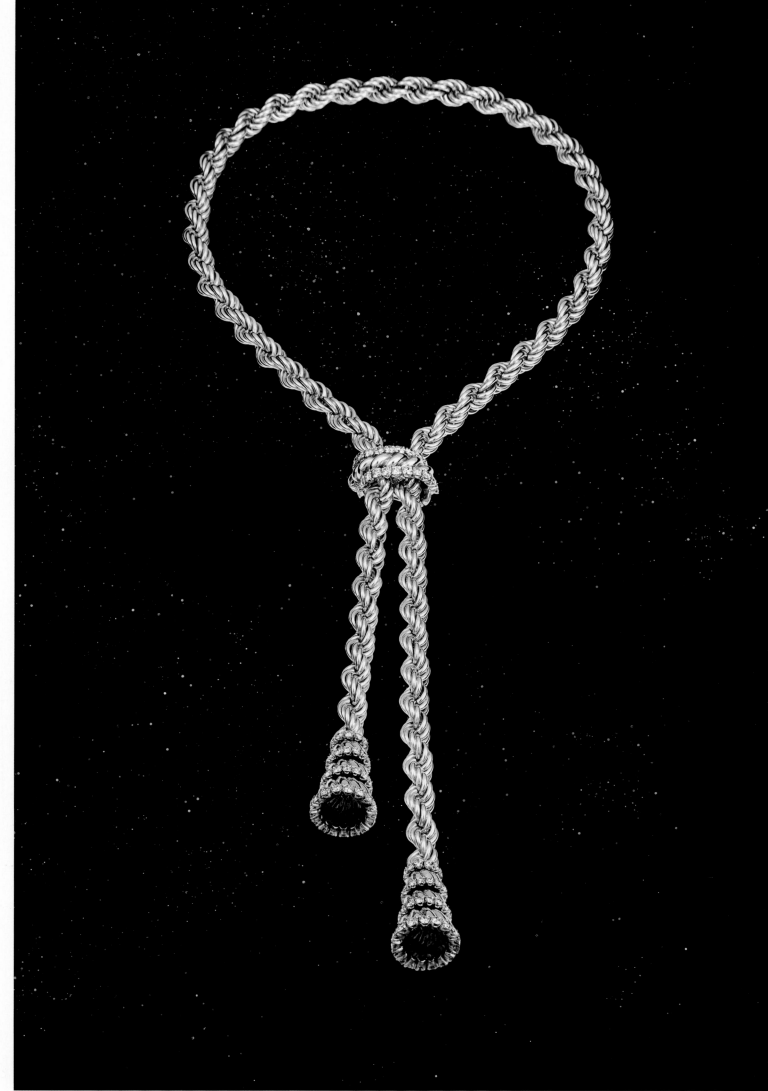

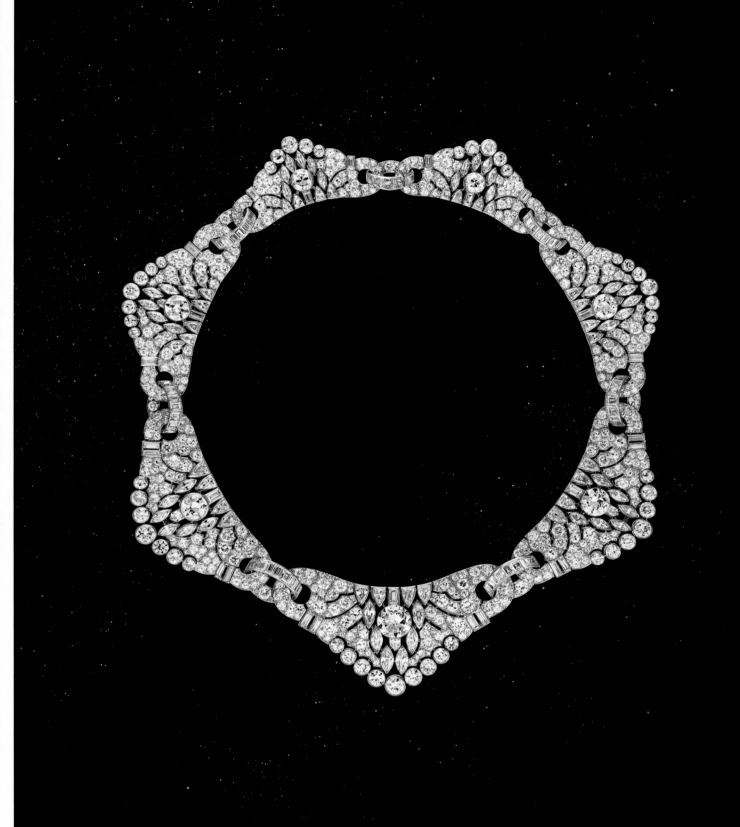

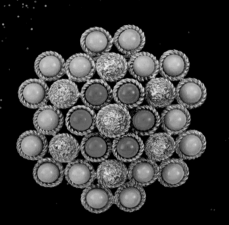

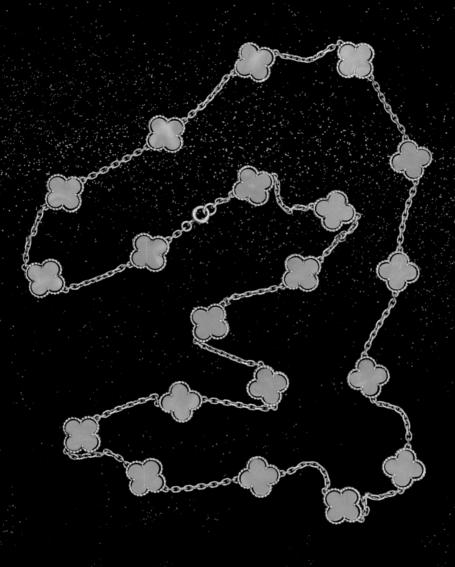

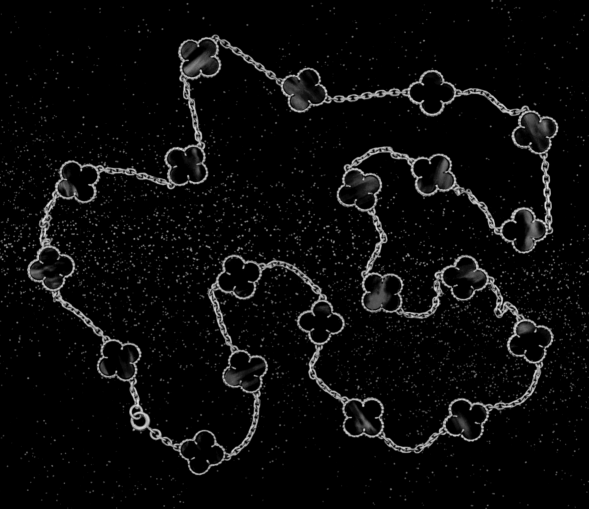

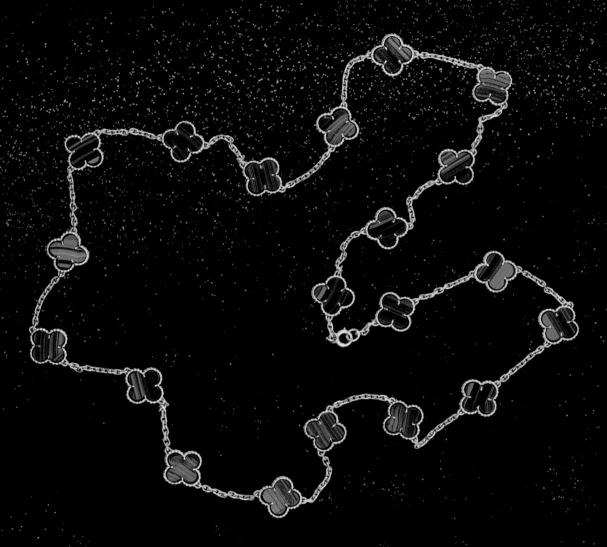

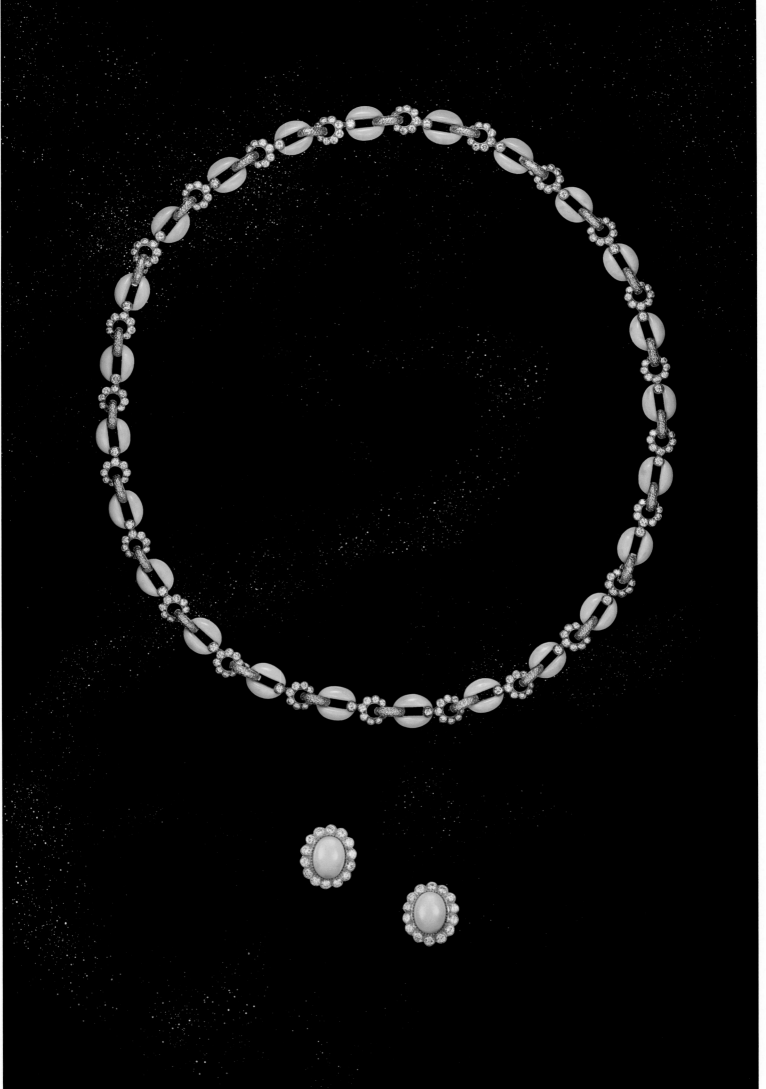

Spirit
of
Exhibition

Dew drops on a branche, drawing by Patrick Jouin.

WHEN I STARTED working on the scenography for *The Spirit of Beauty* exhibition, I rediscovered a jeweller and a world with which I was already familiar: Van Cleef & Arpels had entrusted me with the interior architecture of their historic Place Vendôme boutique in 2006. At the time, I discovered a fabulous universe in which creativity, poetry and craftsmanship go hand in hand, and where every piece of jewellery, whatever its value, is always an open invitation to dream.

For *The Spirit of Beauty*, I, therefore, wanted the visitor to enter this world and forget reality during the time of his or her visit, i.e., one hundred years of jewellery creation. The atmosphere is emphasised by the exhibition's location, since the Mori museum is situated on an extraordinary site which dominates the entire city, giving the impression that it is closer to the heavens than the Earth.

As soon as he or she passes over the threshold of the exhibition, the visitor is plunged into the imaginative world of Van Cleef & Arpels, where nature is at once strong and fragile, alive and pulsating, and from whence fairies and dragonflies arise. The further he or she advances, the deeper the visitor penetrates this nature and the stronger the temptation to lose him- or herself in it, guided by fairies. The latter, which have been a part of the Van Cleef & Arpels universe since the very beginning, are not

Giangantic flotting leaf, drawing by Patrick Jouin.

so much reference points as "emotional guides" that make up this space and help create this emotion.

This magical impression is created by the combination of two elements: scenography and light. As Van Cleef & Arpels wished to present a very large number of pieces, I had to avoid proposing a monolithic presentation system. There are three rooms and thus three different ways of discovering the jewellery, all of which are joined by elements of nature such as drops of water, mist or foliage, in order to create an atmosphere that is both mysterious and simple. It is an organic, sensual and magical blend that allows the visitor not only to see each piece perfectly but also, I hope, to experience an emotion that will help him or her to perceive its beauty. The exhibition is divided into four worlds: "Spirit of Nature" and "Spirit of Elegance", then "Spirit of Adventure" and finally "Incarnations". The visitor wends his or her way through the four themed areas, discovering pieces from different eras that belong to the same theme, assembled in the same show case. Naturally, they are accompanied by explanations that provide not only their date of creation and the stones and metals from which they are crafted, but also the collection from which they are taken and the person who wore them. As for the light, it allows a general ambiance that is both poetic and mysterious to be created. In order to do this, I wanted to create a system that would toy with projected shadows in the form of a butterfly, bird, petal or palm leaf, etc. Light also allows the visitor's gaze to be guided towards a specific area and, of course, reveals the beauty of each piece: the colours and brilliance of the stones, the gold and platinum work, and the art of jewellery creation. Nearly two hundred and fifty pieces are exhibited in this way –some of which belonged to celebrities such as Marlene Dietrich or Grace Kelly, who thus invite us to discover their own particular histories– and which represent beauty in their own way. It is therefore beauty, and its interpretation by Van Cleef & Arpels over the years, that forms the structure of this exhibition. It is this that provides the link between the past, present and future. Of course, it is the retrospective exhibition of a jeweller with a long history, but this history is the fruit of perpetual creative movement and is remade every day.

I would like the visitor who leaves this exhibition, and who departs from this imaginary world to return to reality, to remember the extraordinary work carried out by Van Cleef & Arpels, the incredible cocktail of inventiveness, elegance and beauty of these jewellery creations, and the jeweller's fabulous imaginary world. I would like him or her to leave with a small part of this dream and with the memory of the short moments of eternity and emotion that each of these pieces of jewellery represents.

Patrick JOUIN

Spirit of Nature

13. Mystery Set Bouquet clip
Platinum, rubies, diamonds,
circa 1937
California Collection

13. Mystery Set Disc earrings
Gold, platinum, rubies,
diamonds, 1943
California Collection

14. Clover Bouquet clip
Platinum, diamonds, 1950
Van Cleef & Arpels' Collection

15. Mystery Set Butterfly necklace
Gold, rubies, diamonds, 2003
Private Collection, Japan

16. Mystery Set Three leaves
brooch
Platinum, rubies, diamonds,
1966
Private Collection, New York

17. Mystery Set Vine leaf clip
Gold, platinum, rubies,
diamonds, 1951
Van Cleef & Arpels' Collection

18. Feather brooch
Platinum, diamonds, 1927
Van Cleef & Arpels' Collection

19. Zainabad necklace
Gold, emeralds, diamonds,
2005
Private collection, Hong Kong

20. Mystery Set Chestnut clip
Gold, platinum, sapphires,
diamonds
Formerly His Majesty King
Baudouin's of Belgium
Collection, 1952
Van Cleef & Arpels' Collection

21. Fern clip
Gold, platinum, diamonds,
1959
Van Cleef & Arpels' Collection

22. Art Deco vanity case
Gold, enamel, coral, lapis
lazuli, jade, amethysts,
diamonds, 1926
Hancocks Collection, London

24. Rose's vanity case
Gold, jade, enamel, rubies,
sapphires, emeralds,
diamonds, 1926
Van Cleef & Arpels' Collection

26. Bouquet clip
Gold, moonstones, rubies,
diamonds, 1937
Private Collection

27. Bouquet clip
Gold, sapphires, rubies, 1940
Van Cleef & Arpels' Collection

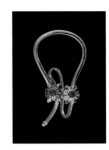

28. Passe-partout jewel
Gold, sapphires, rubies, 1939
Van Cleef & Arpels' Collection

30. Daisy Minaudière
Gold, diamonds, 1950
Van Cleef & Arpels' Collection

32. Daisy Minaudière
Gold, rubies, black lacquer, silk
Former Collection of His
Majesty King Farouk of
Egypt, 1949
Van Cleef & Arpels' Collection

34. Amour en cage necklace and
detachable clip
Gold, Mandarin garnets,
yellow sapphires, 2004
Private Collection, Japan

35. Flower lace bracelet
Gold, rubies, diamonds, 1948
Van Cleef & Arpels' Collection

36. Flower wristwatch
Platinum, diamonds, 1952
Van Cleef & Arpels' Collection

37. Oak leaves watch
Gold, rubies, sapphires,
diamonds, 1951
Van Cleef & Arpels' Collection

38. Bouquet clip
Gold, platinum, rubies,
diamonds, 1937
Van Cleef & Arpels' Collection

39. Daisy clip
Gold, rubies, diamonds, 1964
Van Cleef & Arpels' Collection

40. Mystery Set Violina necklace
Gold, sapphires, white and
yellow diamonds, 2003
Private collection

41. Mystery Set double leaf clip
Platinum, sapphires,
diamonds, 1954
Van Cleef & Arpels' Collection

42. Fairy clip
Gold, diamonds, 2003
Private collection

43. Puck clip
Gold, diamonds, 2003
Private Collection, Japan

44. Ephemere clip
Gold, rubies, sapphires, white
and yellow diamonds, 2008
Private Collection

45. Bunch of grapes clip
Gold, silver, natural pearls,
diamonds, circa 1915
Van Cleef & Arpels' Collection

46. Bird brooch and detachable
briolette yellow diamond
pendant
Gold, sapphire, white and
yellow diamonds, a 95 carats
yellow diamond briolette
Formerly opera singer Ganna
Walska's Collection, 1971
Private Collection, New York

47. Mystery Set Hummingbird box
Yellow, pink and green matte
gold, sapphires, rubies,
diamonds
Former collection of
Her Majesty Queen Nazli of
Egypt, 1938
Van Cleef & Arpels' Collection

48. Mystery Set Platane leaf clip
Gold, platinum, emeralds,
diamonds, 1951
Van Cleef & Arpels' Collection

49. Bird clip
Gold, platinum, sapphires,
rubies, emeralds, diamonds,
1963
Van Cleef & Arpels' Collection

50. Cypress clip
Platinum, diamonds, 1928
Van Cleef & Arpels' Collection

51. Bird brooch
Platinum, rubies, sapphires,
emeralds, onyx, diamonds,
1924
Van Cleef & Arpels' Collection

52. Pylon clips
Gold, sapphires, 1939
California Collection

52. Pylon ring
Gold, sapphires, circa 1939
California Collection

53. Lovebirds clip
Gold, sapphires, rubies,
diamonds, 1946
Van Cleef & Arpels' Collection

54. Mushroom clip
Gold, coral, diamonds, 1968
Van Cleef & Arpels' Collection

55. Orchid brooch
Platinum, diamonds, 1928
Van Cleef & Arpels' Collection

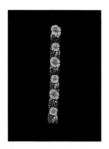

56. Swallow clip
Platinum, diamonds, circa
1928
Van Cleef & Arpels' Collection

57. Bird of paradise hat pin
Platinum, diamonds, 1927
Van Cleef & Arpels' Collection

58. Ear of wheat clip
Platinum, diamonds, 1954
Van Cleef & Arpels' Collection

59. Flowers and leaves bracelet
Platinum, rubies, emeralds,
diamonds, 1937
Zendrini Private Collection

60. Cascade earclips
Platinum, diamonds, 1951
California Collection

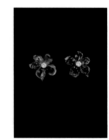

61. Flower basket brooch
Platinum, rubies, emeralds,
diamonds, 1927
Van Cleef & Arpels' Collection

62. Flower clip
Platinum, pearl, diamonds,
1984
Van Cleef & Arpels' Collection

63. Fairy clip
Platinum, rubies, emeralds,
diamonds, circa 1940
Van Cleef & Arpels' Collection

64. Violet clip
Gold, amethysts, diamonds,
1940
Van Cleef & Arpels' Collection

64. Violet earclips
Gold, amethysts, diamonds,
1938
Van Cleef & Arpels' Collection

65. Snowflake clip
Gold, diamonds, 1948
Van Cleef & Arpels' Collection

66. Lovebirds clip
Gold, platinum, rubies,
diamonds, 1945
Van Cleef & Arpels' Collection

66. Lovebirds earrings
Platinum, rubies, diamonds,
1956
Van Cleef & Arpels' Collection

67. Bird brooch
Gold, carved emeralds, rubies,
diamonds, 1964
Faerber Collection

68. Thistle clip
Gold, sapphires, 1937
Van Cleef & Arpels' Collection

69. Table clock
Gold, lapis lazuli, onyx, rock crystal, 1928
Van Cleef & Arpels' Collection

70. Mystery Set Iliade clip
Gold, sapphires, diamonds, 2008
Private collection, Hong Kong

71. Mystery Set Poppy clip
Gold, platinum, rubies, diamonds, 1956
Van Cleef & Arpels' Collection

72. Millefiori vanity case
Platinum, enamel, jasper, diamonds, 1928
Van Cleef & Arpels' Collection

73. Rosace clip
Platinum, diamonds, 1951
Private Collection

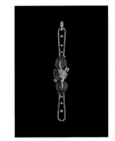

74. Mystery Set Peony clip
Gold, platinum, rubies, diamonds,
Formerly Mahmoud Fakhry Pacha's Collection, 1937
Van Cleef & Arpels' Collection

75. Mystery Set Ruban necklace
Gold, rubies, diamonds, 2008
Private collection

76. Flower watch
Gold, rubies, diamonds, circa 1945
Van Cleef & Arpels' Collection

77. Butterfly clip
Gold, turquoise, rubies, diamonds, 1945
Susan Gale's Collection

78. Leaf wristwatch
Gold, sapphires, diamonds, circa 1950
Van Cleef & Arpels' Collection

79. Buttercup watch
Gold, rubies, 1942
Van Cleef & Arpels' Collection

80. Jardin d'Orient Minaudière
Gold, onyx, coral, jade, aventurine, amazonite, 2006
Private collection, Hong Kong

81. Art Deco bracelet
Platinum, rock crystal, diamonds, circa 1930
Paul Fisher Inc. New York

82. Kikumakie butterfly clip
Gold, wood, diamonds, 2004
Van Cleef & Arpels' Collection

282

Spirit of Elegance

91. Emerald and diamond necklace
*Platinum, emeralds,
diamonds, 1938
Private Collection*

92. Double ribbon clip
*Platinum, diamonds, 1938
Van Cleef & Arpels' Collection*

93. Pampille necklace
*Platinum, pearls, diamonds,
1925
Private Collection*

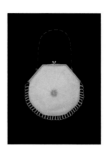

94. Art Deco evening bag
*Platinum, seed pearls,
diamonds, 1924
Van Cleef & Arpels' Collection*

95. Art Deco vanity case
*Gold, natural pearls, black
lacquer, diamonds
Formerly Florence Jay
Gould's Collection, 1925
Van Cleef & Arpels' Collection*

96. Feu follet necklace
*Gold, fancy diamonds, 2002
Private collection, Hong Kong*

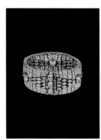

97. Art Deco bracelet
*Platinum, diamonds, 1925
Van Cleef & Arpels' Collection*

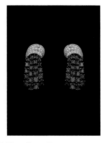

98. Cascade earrings
*Platinum, rubies, diamonds,
1994
Private collection, New York*

99. Cascade necklace
*Platinum, rubies, diamonds,
1993
Private collection, New York*

100. Mystery Set Ludo hexagon
clips
*Gold, rubies, diamonds, 1938
Van Cleef & Arpels' Collection*

100. Mystery Set Ludo hexagon
bracelet
*Gold, rubies, diamonds, 1939
Van Cleef & Arpels' Collection*

101. Tourniquet bracelet watch
*Gold, rubies, diamonds, 1937
Van Cleef & Arpels' Collection*

102. Bow clip
*Platinum, diamonds, 1934
Van Cleef & Arpels' Collection*

103. Pampille earrings
*Platinum, sapphires,
diamonds, 1923
Van Cleef & Arpels' Collection*

104. Ribbon bow clip
*Gold, rubies, diamonds, 1938
Formerly His Highness Prince
Aga Khan's Collection
Van Cleef & Arpels' Collection*

105. Basket weave purse
Gold, diamonds, 1968
European private collection

106. Cigarette case
Gold, rubies, diamonds, 1946
Van Cleef & Arpels' Collection

107. "Empress Eugénie surrounded
by her Ladies", cigarette case
*Gold, rubies, sapphires,
emeralds, diamonds, 1946*
Van Cleef & Arpels' Collection

108. Mystery Set Wild rose
Minaudière
Gold, rubies, 1938
Van Cleef & Arpels' Collection

110. Ribbon bracelet
*Platinum, rubies, diamonds,
1937*
Private Collection

111. Collerette necklace
*Platinum, rubies, diamonds,
1937*
Private Collection

112. Ballerina clips
*Platinum, rubies, emeralds,
diamonds, 1942*
Van Cleef & Arpels' Collection

113. Topaze necklace
*Gold, topazes, diamonds,
1957*
Private Collection, New York

114. Zip bracelet convertible into
a necklace
*Gold, platinum, diamonds,
1951*
Van Cleef & Arpels' Collection

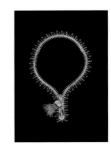

115. Zip necklace convertible into
a bracelet
*Gold, sapphires, rubies,
emeralds, diamonds, 1951*
Private Collection

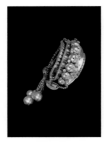

116. Tassel bracelet
Gold, diamonds, 1946
Van Cleef & Arpels' Collection

117. Pampille necklace
*Gold, rubies, diamonds,
circa 1945*
Van Cleef & Arpels' Collection

118. Lace clip
*Gold, platinum, diamonds,
1945*
Van Cleef & Arpels' Collection

119. Lace clip
*Gold, platinum, diamonds,
1949*
Van Cleef & Arpels' Collection

120. Wave bracelet
*Gold, platinum, sapphires,
diamonds, 1937*
Van Cleef & Arpels' Collection

121. Art Deco necklace
Platinum, diamonds, 1928
Private Collection, New York

122. Tassel bracelet
Platinum, diamonds, 1939
California Collection

123. Tassel bracelet
*Platinum, rubies, diamonds,
1929*
Van Cleef & Arpels' Collection

124. Art Deco necklace
Platinum, diamonds, 1927
California Collection

125. Art Deco cigarette case
*Platinum, black lacquer,
diamonds, 1936*
Van Cleef & Arpels' Collection

126. Curl Minaudière
*Gold, platinum, black lacquer,
diamonds, 1935
Van Cleef & Arpels' Collection*

128. Art Deco bracelet
*Platinum, diamonds, 1935
Van Cleef & Arpels' Collection*

129. Zip necklace
*Platinum, gold, diamonds,
2008
California Collection*

130. Mystery Set Ribbon bracelet
*Platinum, sapphires,
diamonds, 1952
Van Cleef & Arpels' Collection*

131. Mystery Set Ludo hexagon
bracelet
*Platinum, sapphires,
diamonds, 1937
Van Cleef & Arpels' Collection*

132. Ludo hexagon bracelet
*Platinum, diamonds, 1937
Van Cleef & Arpels' Collection*

133. Cascatelle necklace
*Gold, emerald, diamonds,
2005
Private collection, Hong Kong*

134. Art Deco pendant earrings
*Platinum, emeralds,
diamonds, 1923
Van Cleef & Arpels' Collection*

135. Art Deco bracelet
*Platinum, rock crystal,
diamonds, 1924
Paul Fisher Inc. New York*

136. Flower Minaudière
*Gold, rubies, black lacquer,
diamonds, 1939
Van Cleef & Arpels' Collection*

137. "Avenue Foch" compact
*Gold, emeralds, rubies,
diamonds, 1945
Van Cleef & Arpels' Collection*

138. Envelope powder compact
*Gold, black enamel, diamonds,
1923
Van Cleef & Arpels' Collection*

139. Vanity case
*Platinum, black enamel, ivory,
diamonds, 1923
Van Cleef & Arpels' Collection*

140. Foliate necklace
*Platinum, gold, rubies,
diamonds, 1959
Private Collection, USA*

141. Bow clip
*Platinum, diamonds, 1928
Van Cleef & Arpels' Collection*

142. Cocktail watch
*Sapphires, natural pearls,
diamonds, 1923
Van Cleef & Arpels' Collection*

143. Band ring
*Platinum, diamonds
Formerly Greta Garbo's
Collection, 1949
Private Collection, USA*

144. Fan clip
*Platinum, rubies, diamonds,
1937
Van Cleef & Arpels' Collection*

145. Mystery Set Wave bracelet
*Platinum, rubies, diamonds,
1936
Van Cleef & Arpels' Collection*

146. Ludo hexagon bracelet
*Platinum, diamonds, 1940
California Collection*

147. Ribbon necklace
Platinum, rubies, diamonds,
1940
Van Cleef & Arpels' Collection

148. Envelope powder compact
Gold, white enamel, 1922
Van Cleef & Arpels' Collection

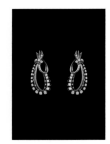

149. Ribbon earclips
Gold, diamonds, 1951
Van Cleef & Arpels' Collection

150. Art Deco evening bag
Gold, rubies, onyx, diamonds,
1929
Van Cleef & Arpels' Collection

151. Natte bracelet
Platinum, diamonds, 1967
New York Collection

152. Bouquet clip
Gold, platinum, rubies,
diamonds, 1941
Van Cleef & Arpels' Collection

153. "Swan lake" compact
Gold, rubies, sapphires,
diamonds, 1947
Van Cleef & Arpels' Collection

154. Manchette bracelet
Platinum, diamonds, 1928
Van Cleef & Arpels' Collection

155. Cadenas wristwatch
Platinum, diamonds, 1940
Van Cleef & Arpels' Collection

156. Envelope powder compact
Gold, black enamel, circa 1922
Van Cleef & Arpels' Collection

157. Fan earclips
Gold, platinum, sapphires,
diamonds, 1935
Formerly Princess of
Kapurthala's Collection
Van Cleef & Arpels' Collection

158. Pearls clip
Platinum, natural pearl,
diamonds, circa 1930
Van Cleef & Arpels' Collection

159. Ballerina clip
Gold, rubies, sapphires,
diamonds, 1944
Van Cleef & Arpels' Collection

159. Ballerina clip
Gold, rubies, turquoise,
diamonds, 1952
Van Cleef & Arpels' Collection

160. Dancer clip
Platinum, sapphire,
diamonds, 1951
Private collection, New York

161. Spanish dancer clip
Gold, platinum, rubies,
emeralds, diamonds, 1941
Van Cleef & Arpels' Collection

161. Ballerina clip
Platinum, emeralds,
diamonds, circa 1940
Van Cleef & Arpels' Collection

161. Ballerina clip
Gold, platinum, rubies,
emeralds, diamonds, 1943
Van Cleef & Arpels' Collection

Spirit
of
Adventure

169. Pagoda pendant brooch
52 Rubies abt. 5.20 cts
platinum, onyx, sapphires,
emeralds, rubies, diamonds,
1924, Siegelson, New York

170. Griffin clip
Gold, enamel, chrysoprase,
lapis lazuli, diamonds, 1972
Van Cleef & Arpels' Collection

171. Griffin clip
Gold, amethysts, emeralds,
carved pink coral, diamonds,
1971
Van Cleef & Arpels' Collection

172. Dragon clip
Gold, emeralds, coral, 1969
Van Cleef & Arpels' Collection

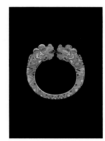

173. Dragon bracelet
Gold, coral, sapphires,
emeralds, diamonds, 1974
Private collection, USA

174. Buddha clip
Platinum, emeralds, rubies,
coral, diamonds, 1927
Van Cleef & Arpels' Collection

175. Siamese head clip
Gold, rubies, sapphires,
emeralds, diamonds, 1968
Van Cleef & Arpels' Collection

176. Egyptian buckle clip
Platinum, rubies, emeralds,
onyx, diamonds, 1925
Van Cleef & Arpels' Collection

177. Japanese scene pendant-brooch
Gold, sapphires, emeralds,
ivory, carved pink tourmaline,
diamonds, 1971
Van Cleef & Arpels' Collection

178. Chinese table clock
Gold, turquoise, onyx, lapis
lazuli, blue enamel, carved
turquoise, 1930
Van Cleef & Arpels' Collection

179. Indian necklace
Gold, carved emerald beads,
rubies and sapphires, 1964
Yafa Signed Jewels New York

180. Buddha watch
Gold, black and green enamel,
1927
Van Cleef & Arpels' Collection

181. Japanese seaside vanity case
Gold, mother-of-pearl, pearl,
enamel, hard stone, diamonds,
circa 1925
Van Cleef & Arpels' Collection

182. Cigarette case
Gold, black and red lacquer,
diamonds, 1935
Van Cleef & Arpels' Collection

183. Fancy bracelet
Yellow gold, sapphires,
emeralds, rubies, diamonds
Former Collection of Marjorie
Merriweather Post, 1942
Van Cleef & Arpels' Collection

184. Bronx cocktail charms bracelet
*Gold, enamels, glass, colored
stones, 1937
Van Cleef & Arpels' Collection*

185. Cambodian clip
*Gold, rubies
Former Collection of Andy
Warhol, 1938
Primavera Gallery, New York*

186. Sautoir and tassel pendant
*Gold, emeralds, rubies,
diamonds, 1974
Zendrini Private Collection*

187. Egyptian bracelet
*Platinum, sapphires, rubies,
emeralds, diamonds, 1924
Van Cleef & Arpels' Collection*

188. Fruit salad bracelet
*Platinum, carved emeralds,
rubies, sapphires, diamonds,
1939
Van Cleef & Arpels' Collection*

189. Indian clip
*Platinum, rubies, sapphires,
emeralds, diamonds, 1924
Van Cleef & Arpels' Collection*

190. Monkey clock
*Gold, amethysts, onyx, amber,
diamonds, 1926
Van Cleef & Arpels' Collection*

191. Coral bracelet convertible
into a necklace
*Gold, coral, diamonds, 1969
The Al Dalaliya collection c/o
Symbolic & Chase*

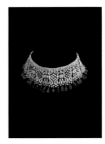

192. Necklace convertible into
two bracelets
*Platinum, emeralds,
diamonds, 1926/1928
California Collection*

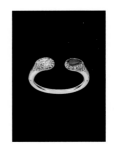

194. Corne d'abondance bracelet
*Platinum, emeralds,
diamonds, 1926
Private Collection*

195. Corne d'abondance bracelet
*Platinum, sapphires,
diamonds, 1924
Private Collection, New York*

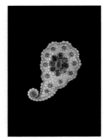

196. Paisley clip
*Gold, rubies, diamonds, 1966
Van Cleef & Arpels' Collection*

197. Basket brooch lapel watch
*Platinum, rubies, sapphires,
emeralds, onyx, diamonds,
1937
Van Cleef & Arpels' Collection*

198. Egyptian purse
*Gold, enamel, diamonds,
silk, 1927
Van Cleef & Arpels' Collection*

199. Egyptian bracelet
*Platinum, emeralds,
sapphires, rubies, diamonds,
circa 1924
Primavera Gallery, New York*

200. Indian necklace
*Gold, carved emeralds,
diamonds, 1971
Formerly Her Highness
Begum Aga Khan's collection
Van Cleef & Arpels' Collection*

201. Art Deco brooch
*Platinum, emeralds,
diamonds, 1928
Van Cleef & Arpels' Collection*

202. Lamp clip
*Platinum, ruby, emeralds,
moonstone, diamonds, 1929
Van Cleef & Arpels' Collection*

203. Buddha clip
*Platinum, gold, emeralds,
sapphires, carved rose quartz,
diamonds, 1978
Van Cleef & Arpels' Collection*

204. Persian cigarette case
*Gold, platinum, amethysts,
black and green enamel,
mother-of-pearl, diamonds,
1927
Van Cleef & Arpels' Collection*

205. Lotus bracelet
Platinum, sapphires,
emeralds, rubies, onyx,
diamonds, 1924
Private Collection, California

206. Peacock box
Gold, green and blue enamel,
circa 1950
Van Cleef & Arpels' Collection

207. Antelope bracelet
Gold, buffalo horn, 1974
Van Cleef & Arpels' Collection

208. Chinese hat set
Gold, 1931
Van Cleef & Arpels' Collection

210. Flower earrings
Gold, amethysts, coral,
diamonds, 1970
Private Collection

211. Flower necklace
Gold, amethysts, coral,
diamonds, 1970
Private Collection

212. Rajah playing luth clip
Gold, rubies, emeralds,
diamonds, 1947
Van Cleef & Arpels' Collection

213. Model of the Varuna yacht
equipped with electrical
contact for a butler's bell.
Gold, silver, enamel, jasper,
ebony, rubies, circa 1908
Van Cleef & Arpels' Collection

214. Chinese landscape lapel watch
Gold, platinum, enamel, cord
Formerly Anna Gould's
Collection, 1924
Van Cleef & Arpels' Collection

215. Ducks table clock
Gold, jade, black enamel,
diamonds, 1930
Van Cleef & Arpels' Collection

216. Blue train vanity case
Platinum, gold, sapphires,
emeralds, diamonds, 1931
Van Cleef & Arpels' Collection

217. Vanity case
Platinum, carved jade, blue
enamel, onyx, diamonds, 1926
Richters of Palm Beach

218. Art Deco mirror
Gold, green lacquer, rose
quartz, nephritis, rubies, 1923
Van Cleef & Arpels' Collection

219. Charms bracelet
Gold, rubies, emeralds,
diamonds, circa 1965
Private Collection, California

220. Cambodian bracelet
Gold, moonstones, rubies,
diamonds, 1937
Private Collection, New York

221. Unicorn clip
Gold, rubies, sapphires,
diamonds, 1950
Private Collection, New York

222. Scylla necklace, detachable clip
Gold, diamonds, 2008
Private Collection, New York

223. Indian embroidery choker
Gold, rubies, emeralds,
diamonds, 1970
Van Cleef & Arpels' Collection

Incarnations

233. Jarretiere bracelet
*Platinum, rubies, diamonds,
circa 1937
Marlene Dietrich's special order
Private Collection, New York*

234. Floating ribbon clip
*worn by Renée Zellweger at
the Bafta Awards ceremony
in London, 2006
Platinum, diamonds, 1937
Van Cleef & Arpels' Collection*

235. Bow clip
*first designed for american
billionaire Barbara Hutton
Platinum, diamonds
Formerly Marquess de
Cuevas' Collection, 1955
Van Cleef & Arpels' Collection*

236. Disc earrings
*Platinum, diamonds, 1934
Formerly Barbara Hutton's
Collection
California Collection*

237. Ludo brick-link
*band bracelet purchased
by Princess Mdivani (more
known under the name of
Barbara Hutton) in 1935
Platinum, diamonds, 1934
Van Cleef & Arpels' Collection*

238. Ruby flower clip
*purchased by opera singer
Maria Callas in 1967.
Platinum, rubies, diamonds,
1967
Van Cleef & Arpels' Collection*

239. Flame clips immortalized by
Jackie Kennedy
*Platinum, diamonds, 1934
Van Cleef & Arpels' Collection*

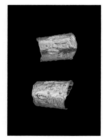

240. Replica of the Etruscan
bracelets from 1973 that
Jackie Kennedy wore in
many occasions
*Hammered gold
Van Cleef & Arpels*

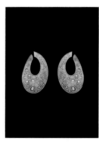

241. Hoop earrings
*Gold, circa 1972
Robin Katz Vintage Jewels*

242. Sautoir necklace
*worn by Liv Tyler at the
ceremony of the Oscars in 2007.
Gold, pink coral, amethysts,
1970
Van Cleef & Arpels' Collection*

243. Chinese hat bracelet
*worn by American actress
Cameron Diaz.
Gold, 1931
Van Cleef & Arpels' Collection*

244. Cambodian bracelet
*worn by Reese Witherspoon
at the ceremony of the
Academy Awards in 2007
Platinum, diamonds, 1938
Van Cleef & Arpels' Collection*

245. Petillantes earrings
*worn by French actress
Carole Bouquet at the Cesar's
ceremony in Paris in 2006
Gold, sapphires, diamonds,
2004
Van Cleef & Arpels*

246. Earrings matching with the
Panka necklace
*Gold, turquoise, diamonds,
1974
Van Cleef & Arpels' Collection*

247. Panka necklace
*worn by Eva Mendes at the
Golden Globes in 2009
Gold, turquoise, diamonds,
1974
Van Cleef & Arpels' Collection*

248. Spirit of beauty fairy clip
bought by Barbara Hutton at Van Cleef & Arpels Beverley Hills boutique in the 40.s
Platinum, rubies, emeralds, diamonds, 1944
Van Cleef & Arpels' Collection

249. Caresse d'Eole necklace
worn by actress Zhang Ziyi at the Cannes Film Festival, 2004
Platinum,diamonds, 2003
Van Cleef & Arpels

250. Ballerina clip
Barbara Hutton owned a similar dancer clip
Gold, rubies, turquoise, 1946
Van Cleef & Arpels' Collection

251. "Rose de Noël" clip
worn by Uma Thurman at the Golden Globes Awards in Los Angeles, 2004
Gold, chalcedony, diamonds, 2000
Van Cleef & Arpels

252. Cotillon earclips
worn by Jessica Alba at the occasion of the Gala Costume Institute in New York, 2009
Gold, emeralds, diamonds, 2009
Van Cleef & Arpels

253. Snowflake necklace
worn by Japanese actress Ryoko Hirosue at the Academy Awards, 2009
Platinum, diamonds, 1986
Van Cleef & Arpels

254. Mimosa earclips
Gold, diamonds, 1948
Fomerly Her Imperial Highness Princess Soraya of Iran's Collection
Van Cleef & Arpels' Collection

255. Mimosa clips
Gold, diamonds, 1948
Fomerly Her Imperial Highness Princess Soraya of Iran's Collection
Van Cleef & Arpels' Collection

256. Cord necklace
Gold, diamonds, 1951
Formerly Her Imperial Highness Princess Soraya of Iran's collection
Van Cleef & Arpels' Collection

257. Lovebirds clip
Gold, rubies, sapphires, diamonds, 1954
Formerly Her Imperial Highness Princess Soraya of Iran's collection
Van Cleef & Arpels' Collection

258. Fan earclips
Platinum, diamonds, 1950
Fomerly Her Imperial Highness Princess Soraya of Iran's Collection
Van Cleef & Arpels' Collection

259. Art Deco necklace
worn by Jennifer Garner at the Academy Awards in 2008.
Platinum, diamonds, 1928
Van Cleef & Arpels' Collection

260. Lotus ring
worn by actress Anne Hathaway at the Gala Costume Institute in New York, 2009
Gold, diamonds, 2001
Van Cleef & Arpels

261. Tiara
worn by Her Serene Highness Princess Grace of Monaco
Gold, platinum, diamonds, 1976
Van Cleef & Arpels' Collection

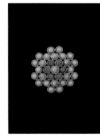

262. Cabochon brooch
Gold, chrysoprase, coral, 1972
Private collection of Her Serene Highness Princess Grace of Monaco, Principality of Monaco

263. Vintage Alhambra necklace
Gold, coral, 1973
Private collection of Her Serene Highness Princess Grace of Monaco, Principality of Monaco

264. Vintage Alhambra necklace
Gold, tortoiseshell, 1971
Private collection of Her Serene Highness Princess Grace of Monaco, Principality of Monaco

265. Vintage Alhambra necklace
Gold, malachite, 1975
Private collection of Her Serene Highness Princess Grace of Monaco, Principality of Monaco

266. Beauty case
Gold, crystal, tortoiseshell, velvet, silk, leather, 1958
Private collection of Her Serene Highness Princess Grace of Monaco, Principality of Monaco

267. Hedgehog brooch
Gold, turquoise, rubies, 1960
Private collection of Her Serene Highness Princess Grace of Monaco, Principality of Monaco

268. Coral ring
Gold, coral, diamonds, 1981
Private collection of
Her Serene Highness
Princess Grace of Monaco,
Principality of Monaco

269. Coral sautoir
Gold, coral, diamonds, 1976
Private collection of
Her Serene Highness
Princess Grace of Monaco,
Principality of Monaco

269. Coral earrings
Gold, coral, diamonds, 1981
Private collection of
Her Serene Highness
Princess Grace of Monaco,
Principality of Monaco

270. Butterfly clip
Gold, turquoise, rubies,
diamonds, 1961
Private collection of
Her Serene Highness
Princess Grace of Monaco,
Principality of Monaco

Contributors

Van Cleef & Arpels wishes to extend particular thanks to

Francois CURIEL

François Curiel is a leading figure in the international auction world. Chairman of Christie's in Europe, he is a reputed specialist responsible for Christie's global jewellery sales and has been described in the press as one of the ten greatest auctioneers of our time. In 1996, he was awarded the prestigious Antwerp Diamond Career Award from the Diamond High Council in Belgium and in January 2009, he was promoted Officer of the French Legion of Honor.

Patrick GRIES

Photographer Patrick Gries is renown for his work in the realms of art, luxury goods, and design. He is co-author of several books including *Évolution* and *Franck Sorbier, la couture corps et âme* published by Éditions Xavier Barral; as well as *Andrea Branzi Open Enclosures*, *Nature démiurge* and *César* for Fondation Cartier Paris and *Madeleine Vionnet* for Musée des Arts Décoratifs Paris. This project has been realized in collaboration with Xavier Barral.

Vincent MEYLAN

Vincent Meylan is a french journalist and a writer. For 20 years, he has been specialized in royal families and jewellery, being in charge for the magazine *Point de vue* of the special luxury editions. He is knowledgeable in all aspects of French art de vivre, savoir faire and culture. He has written three biographies and two books about jewellery.

Laurence MOUILLEFARINE

Laurence Mouillefarine a freelance journalist specializing in the art market and collecting, is a contributing editor at *Madame Figaro* and *AD*. She is co-author, with Véronique Ristelhueber, of *Raymond Templier*, the first monograph of the jeweller (Norma éditions, 2005). In spring 2009, she was co-curator of the exhibition *Bijou Art déco and Avant-garde*, at the Musée des Arts Décoratifs in Paris.

Janet ZAPATA

Janet Zapata is an independent scholar and museum consultant, specializing in jewelry and silver. She is a frequent contributor to *Art & Antiques* and *The Magazine Antiques* and has written several books including *The Jewelry and Enamels of Louis Comfort Tiffany and The Art of Zadora: America's Faberge*. She curated the exhibitions *The Nature of Diamonds and Tiffany: 150 Years of Gems and Jewelry* at the American Museum of Natural History in New York City and *The Glitter and the Gold: Fashioning America's Jewelry* at the Newark Museum.

Exhibition

Van Cleef & Arpels – *The Spirit of Beauty*

Mori Arts Center Gallery
October 31, 2009 – January 17, 2010
Organizers: The Asahi Shimbun, TBS
With the Special Cooperation of: Van Cleef & Arpels
Concept-Designer: Patrick Jouin
In Association with The French Embassy

Aknowledgments

Van Cleef & Arpels particularly wants to thank and express his deepest gratitude to:

All the friends and clients who have loved and worn its unique creations for over a century.
The Maison also wishes to give homage to all the colleagues in France, and throughout the world,
whose passion and talent have always contributed to its renown.

The lenders of essential pieces which complement
the objects from the Van Cleef & Arpels collection:

Stephen Burton
Lucille and Milton Coleman
Ralph Esmerian
Thomas Faerber
Paul Fisher
Elliot Friman
Susan Gale,
Robin Katz
Audrey Friedman and Haim Manishevitz
Maurice Moradof
Stefan Richter and Dudley Richter,
Lee Siegelson
Suzanne Tennenbaum
Martin Travis
Jay Waldmann
Carlo Zendrini
and all the other anonymous lenders

The Van Cleef and Arpels' family

The Principality of Monaco
His Serene Highness Prince Albert II of Monaco
Hervé Irien
Carl de Lencquesaing

Catherine Deneuve

Patrick Jouin
Élodie Martin

Alain Szabason
Benoît Ageron
Machida Yoshio

Lisa Hubbard, Sotheby's
Gabriella Mantegani, Sotheby's
Helen Molesworth, Christie's
Steven Neckman
Natacha Vassiltchikov, Christie's
Claire de Truchis Lauriston, Sotheby's

Xavier Barral and his team

VAN CLEEF & ARPELS INTERNATIONAL

Stanislas de Quercize, President & CEO
Nicolas Bos, Vice President & Creative Director
Catherine Cariou, Heritage Director
Laëtitia Abdelli
Vanessa Angleys
Clémentine Charrier
Solène Desgrees Du Lou
Frédéric Gilbert-Zinck
Isabelle Godard
Sibylle Jammes
Elise Gonnet
Sibylle Jammes
Antoine Lacroix
Valentine Lepeu
Béatrice Le Metayer
Claire Masquelier
Jean-Jacques Masson
Virginie Matras-Joly
Frédéric Morales
Laetitia Paute
Gwenaëlle Petit-Pierre
Sita de Sarila
Delphine Thabard

VAN CLEEF & ARPELS JAPAN

Yoshiko Saito, Marketing & Communication Director
Masahiko Tsunoda, Exhibition Project Manager
Minako Iikura
Kumiko Homma
Daisuke Murakami
Mie Suzuki
Chiaki Kitahara, Exhibition Project Coordinator
Mathias Ortmann
Vincent Nilins, Retail Director
Clémentine Climent
Mélanie Saga

VAN CLEEF & ARPELS INC.

Nicolas Luchsinger,
Store Director New York
Kristina Buckley
Cindy Prasnal
Inezita Gay
Catherine Harrison

RICHEMONT JAPAN

Tomohiro Oka
Mikiko Isozaki
Kango Harauchi

Art director, publication editor
Xavier Barral

Editorial coordinator
Michel Baverey

Graphic design and production
Atalante-Paris
www.atalante-paris.fr

Assistants for photographies
Thomas Gauthier
Ji-Yun Lim

© Éditions Xavier Barral for this edition
ISBN 978 2915173 54 3
Registration: October 2009

Éditions Xavier Barral
42, rue Sedaine, 75011 Paris, France
www.exb.fr

Printed in October 2009 by imprimerie des Deux Ponts, France